# JUNIOR
# ENCYCLOPEDIA

Our Universe

STERLING

# JUNIOR
# ENCYCLOPEDIA

## Our Universe

STERLING

**Sterling Publishers Private Limited**

A-59, Okhla Ind. Area, Phase II, New Delhi-110020. India
Tel: 91-11-26386165; Fax: 91-11-26383788
E-mail: mail@sterlingpublishers.com
Website: www.sterlingpublishers.com

*Junior Encyclopedia - Our Universe*
© 2012, Sterling Publishers Private Limited

*Printed at Sterling Publishers Pvt. Ltd, New Delhi*

# Contents

| | |
|---|---|
| Introduction | 11 |
| Universe | 12 |
| Planets | 18 |
| Space Exploration | 64 |
| Earth | 84 |
| Landforms | 88 |
| Weather, Climate, Earthquakes & Volcanoes | 110 |
| Discoveries and Inventions | 180 |

# Introduction

What do you see when you look around you? City streets, open country, rolling hills or the sea? The environment that we live in depends on its position in the Universe, the rock that lies beneath the land, its climatic changes and the changes that people have made to it. Millions of years have shaped and formed our world – through evolution and transformations undergone by the features that make up our landscape.

Approach the marvels of the sky with its mysteries, explore the wonderful home that shelters all the living beings – plants and animals alike, whose relationship with the environment is an essential part of the Earth's ecological balance, learn about the varied weather patterns and finally mankind's greatest discoveries, charting the world around him towards outer space as well as around the Earth and the wonderful creations that have made life better!

# UNIVERSE

Ever since the beginning of human evolution, people have been curious about the world that surrounds them. As their knowledge increased, these surroundings expanded to include the heavens. In an attempt to make sense of them, people devised scientific and religious theories. Each new explanation presented new problems. Today we are beginning to have a more accurate idea of how the universe originated.

# The Universe and the Solar System

## Origin of the Universe

Astronomers' believe that about 15 billion years ago there was an explosion of unimaginable size. A mass of tremendous density, in which the atoms were packed tightly together, exploded. This event is referred to as the big bang. The force it unleashed scattered the dense material in all directions at a speed approaching that of light. With time, as the masses of this material got farther away from the centre of the explosion and slowed down, material that was close together formed galaxies.

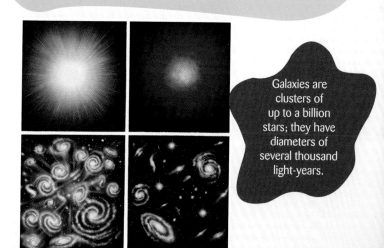

Galaxies are clusters of up to a billion stars; they have diameters of several thousand light-years.

## Our Galaxy: The Milky Way

Among the many galaxies that make up the universe, the one we know best is the Milky Way, since that is where we are located. On a dark night when the sky is clear, a faint white band can be seen stretching across the sky from horizon to horizon. That is the Milky Way. The famous astronomer, Galileo, was the first person to look closely at the Milky Way through a telescope.

By looking at the white band of the Milky Way, astronomers have worked out that our Sun and its planetary system belong to the Milky Way. The Sun is one of the 100,000 million stars which make up the Milky Way.

### What is a Light Year?

A light year is a measure of distance and not of time. Light travels at a speed of 300,000 km/second. Considering this, the distance that light will travel in one year is taken to be one light year. This equals to 9.461X1012 km. The mean distance between the Sun and the Earth is 149,598,000 km. In terms of light years, it is 8.311.

# Comets

A comet is a heavenly body that has a very distinct appearance and behaviour, and that travels through the solar system.

## Meteorite Showers

When the tail of comet comes close to the Earth, a very striking phenomenon is produced, known as a meteorite shower. A great number of falling stars – far greater than normal – enter the night sky. Any meteoroid that comes into contact with the atmosphere turns into a shooting star when it disintegrates. Some showers of shooting stars occur at fixed times due to the fact that the Earth crosses the former path of a comet.

# Eclipses

Eclipses are a phenomenon that is a product of the celestial workings, when two or more heavenly bodies line up in certain positions in their orbits, thereby interfering with the light that carries from one to another.

## Lunar Eclipse

When the full Moon passes through the shadow of the earth, it forms what is known as a lunar eclipse. During a lunar eclipse, the moon usually turns red in colour. There are at least 2 eclipses of the Moon every year, each eclipse lasting up to an hour and a half.

It is not dangerous at all to look at a lunar eclipse because the moon does not make its own light.

### Did you know...?

Ancient Greek astronomers concluded that the earth was round when they saw the earth's shadow during the occurrence of a lunar eclipse.

## Solar Eclipse

A Solar Eclipse occurs when the moon comes in between the Sun and the Earth. The Moon blocks most of the sunlight from entering the earth thereby turning day into night for a few minutes in the area where the Solar Eclipse is occurring. During a total eclipse, a ring of light around the moon can be seen from the Earth.

Looking at a Solar Eclipse directly can cause blindness. That is why there are special glasses that protect the eyes from radiation.

Solar eclipses cover a smaller area of the surface of the Earth, so they can be observed only from certain places,

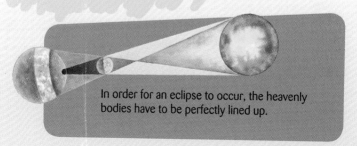

In order for an eclipse to occur, the heavenly bodies have to be perfectly lined up.

# PLANETS

The Earth is a small planet which revolves around the Sun, one of the 100 billion stars in our galaxy. Other planets move around the Sun, captives of its gravitational pull. Almost all the planets have moons around them. This group, along with a multitude of smaller bodies, together make up the Solar System.

# The Solar System

Among the thousands of stars that make up the Milky Way the Sun is a medium-sized star located on the edge of the galaxy. This unique star and the planets that revolve around it make up what we call the Solar System. It comprises eight planets, their moons, and a band of rocky remains that form what is known as the Asteroid Belt. The Asteroid Belt sits between the orbits of the planets Jupiter and Mars.

## Planets of the Solar System

The outer planets – Jupiter, Saturn, Uranus and Neptune are different from the inner planets – Mercury, Venus, Earth and Mars. The former group of planets, also known as jovian (Jupiter-like) planets are large and gaseous while the inner or terrestrial (Earth-like) planets are usually smaller and mainly rocky.

## What is the reason for this difference?

The inner planets were formed close to the Sun, where it was too hot for the gases to condense to solid particles. And the solar wind, being most intense near the Sun blew off lots of gases and dust from the inner planets, making them rocky. Further away from the Sun, the solar winds were not intense enough to cause similar removal of gases from the outer planets. Also, the inner planets being smaller with lower gravity could not hold the escaping gases.

# Solar System: Evolution

The formation of the Solar System is believed to have begun billions and billions of years ago. Before the Solar System came into existence, scientists believe that there was a giant cloud of dust and gas. This massive cloud was believed to have been disturbed probably by the explosion of a nearby star. This caused the dust and gas to collapse due to the pull of gravity. As it did so, it began spinning in a giant circle. It grew hotter and denser at the centre.

At the centre of this rotating cloud, a small star came to be formed. This star grew bigger and bigger, collecting more dust and more gas. This star became the Sun.

## Did you know...?

The Sun is more than 4 billion years old!

Further away, smaller clumps of dust and gas left over from the Sun's formation were also collapsing. The dust the scientists believed evolved from dead stars. These clumps soon formed into eight planets, orbiting the hotter and denser star – the Sun. These planets were thus named – Mercury, Venus, Earth, Mars, Jupiter, Saturn, Uranus and Neptune.

### Did you know…?

The Solar system has over 100 Worlds!

While there are only eight planets orbiting the Sun, the Solar System has other worlds. There are dwarf planets, moons, comets and asteroids just as fascinating. Some of these dwarf planets and moons have lakes, rivers, oceans and even volcanoes. Some are even larger than Jupiter, the biggest planet on our Solar System.

Just as the planets were formed, so also were the dwarf planets, moons, comets and asteroids formed. These together with the Sun and the eight planets form the Solar System.

A planet is a large space object that orbits or revolves around a star, also reflecting that star's light.
The solar system is made up of several small systems known as planetary systems. Every one of these systems is made up of a planet and one or more moons revolving around it. Out of all the planets that orbit the Sun in our Solar System, planets Mercury and Venus are the only two that do not have moons.

# lanets of our Solar System

Mercury is the innermost and smallest planet in the Solar System. It is a small rocky planet which is covered with craters.

Venus is the second planet from the Sun. It is the sixth largest planet in our Solar System.

Earth is the third planet from the Sun, and the densest and fifth largest of the eight planets. Earth is the only planet known to sustain life.

Mars is the fourth planet from the Sun in the Solar System and the seventh largest of the eight planets.

Jupiter is the fifth planet from the Sun and the largest planet within the Solar System.

Saturn is the sixth planet from the Sun and the second largest planet in the Solar System.

Uranus is the seventh planet in the Solar System. It is the third largest planet in the Solar System.

Neptune is the eighth and last planet in the Solar System. It is the fourth largest planet and third heaviest.

## Did you know?

Many years ago, Pluto was considered to be a planet. Pluto was considered to be the ninth planet which was furthest from the Sun. But later on Pluto was thought to be too small to be categorised as a 'planet'. So in 2006, Pluto was categorised as a dwarf planet.

# Classification of Planets

## Dwarf Planets

Ceres, Pluto, Haumea, Makemake and Eris.

Dwarf planets are round objects orbiting the sun. They are similar to the Solar System's eight planets, but they are smaller in size and are not moons. This term was created in the year 2006 after the discovery of smaller planets in our solar system. Pluto, Ceres, Haumea, Eris and Makemake are the first three members classified as dwarf planets. Hundreds more are yet to be identified.

## Gaseous Planets

The gaseous planets are mostly made up of gases, mainly hydrogen and helium as the main part of their composition. They are mostly surrounded by rings and have many moons.

Jupiter, Saturn, Uranus and Neptune.

## Rocky Planets

The rocky planets are mostly made up of rock and metal. These planets are very heavy and move slowly. They also do not have rings and very few moons.

Mercury, Venus, Earth, Mars.

**Mercury** - Closest planet to the Sun.
**Venus** - The hottest planet
**Earth** - Our home planet.
**Mars** - Closest planet to the Earth
**Jupiter** - Largest planet of solar system
**Saturn** - Giant rings surrounding the planet.
**Uranus** - Sideways Planet.
**Neptune** - The farthest planet from the Sun.

### Did you know?

- The Sun is so large that it could fit a million earths inside it.

- There are countless other stars like the sun with planets, moons, comets and many other fascinating objects that revolve around it in the Universe.

# Mercury

Slightly larger than the Moon, this inner planet is the smallest one and closest to the Sun. It has no moons orbiting around it. Its orbit is oval and its surface is full of craters. Temperatures on Mercury are extremely high and there is no atmosphere.

In Roman mythology Mercury is the god of commerce, travel and thievery. Mercury is also known as Hermes, the messenger of the Gods, in Greek mythology.

The largest of Mercury's craters, also the largest in the Solar System is the one designated Caloris Basin, measuring about 1,550 km in diameter.

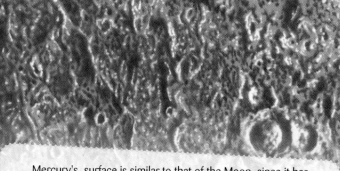

Mercury's surface is similar to that of the Moon, since it has numerous craters caused by the impact of meteorites. The craters have been safe from erosion because Mercury has no atmosphere. The reason for this absence of atmosphere is that the force of the planet's gravitational pull is too weak to retain atmospheric gases.

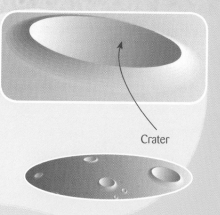

Some of Mercury's craters are filled with ice because the sun never reaches into the shadows.

Crater

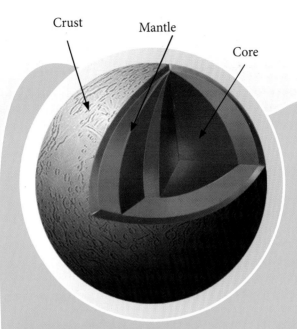

Crust

Mantle

Core

## Inside Mercury

**Crust:** The crust is solid shell that surrounds the mantle. It is almost 100-300 km thick.

**Mantle:** It is a thick shell, almost 500-700 km thick, which surrounds the core of the Mercury.

**Core:** Core of the Mercury is very hot and it is mostly composed of iron-nickel.

Average distance from the Sun: 58 million km (0.39 times that of Earth)

Length of year: 0.24 Earth years

Length of a day: 59 Earth day

Diameter: 4,878 km (0.38 times that of Earth)

It is difficult to observe this small planet from Earth because of its orbit and its proximity to the Sun. It is visible to observers on Earth in the late evenings or early morning sky.

No one knew much about this planet until the year 1974. In that year, spaceship Mariner X passed near the planet and took many photographs that revealed Mercury's landscape is similar to that of the moon.

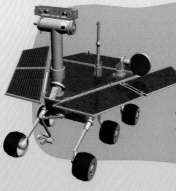

In March 2011, the spacecraft Messenger became the first to orbit the planet. Photographs taken by the spacecraft, Messenger show that the planet is marked with great cliffs and an uneven landscape while a major part of its surface is covered in plains.

# Venus

Venus has no moons.

The spacecrafts that have landed on Venus have shown that its surface is very uneven. It is covered with craters that are very large in size. There are many major volcanoes on Venus that show it is a volcanically active planet. Many areas of Venus are covered in lava.

## Did you know?

It was believed for a long time, before its characteristics were fully known, that the planet could sustain life. But it was later discovered that the surface temperature was too high.

The first spacecraft to visit Venus was Mariner 2 in 1962. Venus has since been visited by more than 20 spacecrafts!

After the Moon, it is the brightest natural object in the night sky.

Average distance from the Sun: 108 million km (0.72 times that of Earth)

Length of year: 0.62 Earth years

Length of a day: 243 Earth days

Venus' surface cannot be observed directly because the planet is permanently covered by a thick layer of clouds.

There are mountains higher than Everest on Venus, and land formations that remind us of the continents on Earth, rising above the average level of the planet. Among them are great depressions that may at one time have been ocean beds, which evaporated long ago.

35

Venus is often called Earth's twin because it is the closest planet in size to Earth.

## Structure of the Planet

Venus is a solid planet made up of a core of a metallic nature, surrounded by a very thick rocky mantle and crust. Splace probes that have succeeded in landing on the surface have shown a landscape with broad plains, deep valleys, and mountains exceeding 10,000m in height. The deep depressions seem to be the remains of seas that must have existed before the present thick atmosphere was fromed.

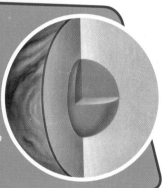

The atmosphere of Venus consists of 96 per cent carbon dioxide; the rest is made up of nitrogen, water vapour, sulphur dioxide, and lesser quantities of other chemical compounds.

Venus' surface is very hot - about 400 degrees Celsius!

Venus is the Roman goddess of love and beauty. She is known as Aphrodite in Greek mythology.

The interior of Venus is almost similar to that of Earth.

Venus is constantly covered by thick clouds of sulphuric acid. Due to the presence of these thick clouds neither Sun nor Earth are visible from its surface.

## Did you know?

Venus' hot temperature is due to what we call "the Greenhouse Effect." The large amount of carbon dioxide in Venus' atmosphere acts like a blanket. The heat gets trapped underneath the thick layer of clouds. Because the heat has nowhere to go, Venus gets hotter and stays hot.

# Earth

Of all the planets that make up the Solar system, the Earth is the only one that supports life. This is a planet where the surface temperatures remain moderate because of the presence of water and an atmosphere.

The Earth isn't perfectly round. It is slightly flattened at the north and south poles.

Temperatures at the Earth's centre or the "core" may be as high as 7500 K – hotter than the surface of the Sun!

Earth is also the largest of the Solar System's four terrestrial planets.

Astronauts have always described the Earth as the blue planet. The oceans and the gases in the atmosphere are responsible for this colour. The water and the air are what makes life possible on Earth and are unique in the whole Solar System.

The Earth is in constant motion. Along with the rest of the planets, plus the Sun, it moves throughout our galaxy, but that does not affect us in our daily lives. It is of greater significance for us that it spins on its axis, producing day and night, and that it revolves around the Sun, making the seasons.

Average distance from the Sun: 150 million km

Diameter: 12,104 km

Distance from the Earth to the Moon: 384,400 km

The Earth is the densest of all the planets in the solar system. This means that it's the most "compact" of all the planets.

# Mars

This planet is one of the most noticeable ones because of its reddish color. It is smaller than the Earth; its surface is covered with large rocky and sandy plains, with mountains and small craters. It has a very thin atmosphere, and there are considerable expanses of ice in the polar regions that vary with the time of year.

For a long time, it was thought that Mars, the red planet, was inhabited by "martians." It was later confirmed that there is infact no intelligent life on Mars.

Mars has two tiny moons which orbit very close to the surface. Their names are Phobos and Deimos.

Phobos
Deimos
Mars

**Phobos**
It is larger of the two moons. It is small and irregular shaped object and least reflective body in solar system.

**Deimos**
It is the outermost moon of Mars.

Mars has permanent ice caps at both poles made up mostly of solid carbon dioxide. We know this as "dry ice."

One of the most important features of this planet is the great storms that occur, stirring up great quantities of dust. In 1971, dust storms covered the whole planet from view!

Mars is the god of war. In Greek mythology, he is known as Ares.

Mars is sometimes referred to as the "Red Planet" due to the iron oxide prevalent on its surface.

Ice on Mars

The first spacecraft to visit Mars was Mariner 4 in 1965. Several others followed including the two Viking landers in 1976. After a long break, Mars Pathfinder landed successfully on Mars on July 4, 1997.

Olympus Mons is the largest mountain in the Solar System. Olympus Mons rises a full 24 km above the surrounding plain. Its base is more than 500 km across and is rimmed by a cliff 6 km (20,000 ft) high.

Hellas Planitia is a huge crater in the southern hemisphere. It's over 6 km deep and 2000 km across.

Valles Marineris is a network of canyons that runs 4000 km long and stands from 2 to 7 km tall.

Of all the planets in the Solar System, the one that has the best conditions to sustain life is Mars. Still, this would require much effort, since, among other things, it has no breathable atmosphere.

# Jupiter

Jupiter is so big that you could cram 1,000 Earths inside of it!

Jupiter is the giant of the Solar System. Its diameter is ten times greater than the Earth's. Its gravitational pull is so high, that it slightly affects the movement of all other planets.

Jupiter's most outstanding and interesting feature is called "The Great Red Spot." The Great Red Spot is an oval about 12,000 km by 25,000 km, resembling a hurricane! It is thought that Jupiter's "Great Red Spot" is a storm of swirling gas that has lasted for hundreds of years.

Jupiter was the King of the Roman Gods. To the ancient Greeks, he was known as Zeus, ruler of the Greek Gods and Mount Olympus.

Jupiter was first visited by the Pioneer 10 spacecraft in 1973. It was later visited by Pioneer 11, Voyager 1, Voyager 2 and Ulysses.

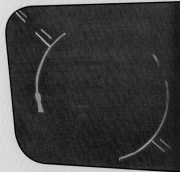

Interplanetary probes Pioneer and Voyager captured photographs of Jupiter when they passed by it during their journey to the outer planets. On the Voyager probe travels it captured images of Jupiter's dark side, where a thick ring surrounding the planet can be seen.

Jupiter has 16 known moons! There are four large "Galilean" moons, and 12 small ones. With a small telescope they can easily be observed from the Earth.

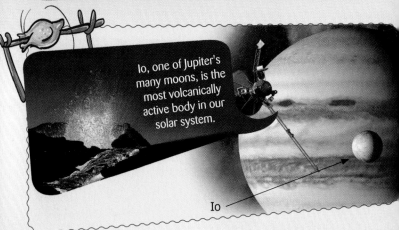

Io, one of Jupiter's many moons, is the most volcanically active body in our solar system.

Io

Jupiter has faint rings like Saturn's, but much smaller. Unlike Saturn's, Jupiter's rings are dark. They're probably composed of very small grains of rocky material.

Jupiter's moon Europa appears very bright, which suggests a surface covered with ice. Europa has linear features, which are said to be caused by cracks in a sheet of ice, floating on a subsurface.

Ganymede is the largest moon in the Solar System.

### Did you know?

Like Earth and many other planets, Jupiter acts like a giant magnet. Jupiter's magnetic field is about 14 times as strong as Earth's.

# Saturn

## Did you know?

If we were to put Saturn in a bathtub full of water, it would float! The only problem is finding a bathtub big enough.

Saturn has long-lived "spots" as well.

Saturn's magnificent rings make this planet unmistakable. Even with a small telescope it is possible to see the little disk of Saturn surrounded by its rings. Saturn seems so small when seen from the Earth because it is almost twice as far away as Jupiter.

48

Saturn was first visited by the Pioneer 11 spacecraft in 1979. Saturn has also since been visited by Voyager 1 and Voyager 2.

**Did you know?**

The name 'Saturn' came from the English word, 'Saturday.'

In Roman mythology, Saturn is the god of agriculture. He is known as Cronus in Greek mythology. Cronus was the father of Zeus (Jupiter).

Saturn's rings can be seen easily from Earth with a small telescope. Yet every 15 years they stop being visible. It is then while in its orbit around the Sun, Saturn's position is such that the rings become very thin.

Saturn's rings, unlike the rings of the other gas planets, are very bright. Though they look "solid" or continuous from the Earth, the rings are actually composed of many, many small particles circling Saturn at their own speeds.

Saturn's rings are made up mostly of water ice, but they may also include rocky particles with icy coatings.

Saturn's rings are extraordinarily thin. Even though they measure about 250,000 km across, they're no more than 1.5 km thick.

Saturn's ring system is one of the most spectacular phenomena of the Solar System. The thickness of the different fringes or rings is only a few miles. Each ring is formed by a great number of ice particles. These celestial bodies rotate around the planet.

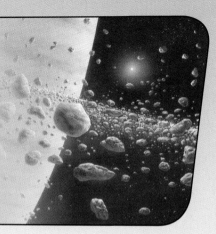

Saturn has 18 known moons plus some more smaller ones that are part of the rings.

The largest of all is Titan, at 5,150 km in diameter; it is located at a median distance of 1,222,000 km from Saturn.

The moon Mimas measures 392 km in diameter and has a tremendous crater 100 km in diameter, the result of an impact from a meteorite.

# Uranus

Uranus has been visited by only one spacecraft, Voyager 2 on Jan 24, 1986.

Uranus has twenty seven known moons.

Uranus was unknown in ancient times, and was the first planet to be discovered with a telescope. In fact, it can be seen with the naked eye, but without a big telescope, you wouldn't be able to distinguish the planet's disk.

One of its notable characteristics is that its rotation axis lies on the plane of its orbit around the Sun. Uranus is also, next to Saturn, the first planet where rings were discovered.

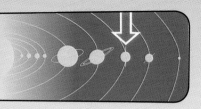

Uranus is the seventh planet from the Sun and the third largest of the eight planets.

Uranus is the ancient Greek God of the Heavens - the earliest supreme god. He was the father of Cronus and of the Cyclopes and Titans.

In 1986 the spaceship Voyager 2 came close enough to photograph the rings of the planet. They are a series of ten thin rings made up of small fragments of rock and other very dark matter.

## URANUS' FIVE MAJOR MOONS

Five Moons belonging to Uranus have been observed from the Earth, but little can be learned about them from such a great distance. *Voyager* observed them in detail and also discovered ten new moons.

**Miranda:** smallest of all five moons with canyons much deeper than Grand Canyon

**Ariel:** youngest moon

**Umbriel:** brightest of all moons, mysterious bright ring on one side

**Oberon:** heavily cratered

**Titania:** largest of Uranus' moon, made up of half ice and half rock

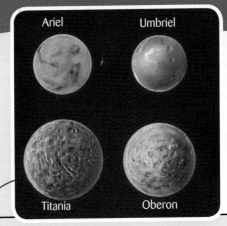

The four largest Moons of Uranus, from left to right and top to bottom: Ariel 1,160 km, Umbriel 1,170 km, Titania 1,580 km and Oberon 1,520 km.

Uranus' blue colour is the result of a gas called "methane" found in the planet's upper atmosphere.

Like the other gas planets, Uranus has bands of clouds that blow around rapidly. Uranus' bands are very, very faint.

On Uranus, the south and north poles get 42 years of constant day and 42 years of constant night.

Miranda is the strangest-looking Uranian moon, appearing as though it were made of spare parts.

Uranus spins differently from most planets. It seems to be tilted "sideways" instead of right side up.

The planet is probably made up a rocky core surrounded by a thick mantle of ice, topped off by the gaseous atomsphere.

55

# Neptune

Neptune was the first planet located through mathematical predictions rather than through regular observations of the sky.

Neptune orbits the sun once every 165 years.

Neptune is a blue gaseous planet that can be seen only with the aid of powerful binoculars. It has a very active atmosphere, as indicated by its spots and transverse bands. It is surrounded by a small ring.

Neptune is the coldest planet in the Solar System as it is farthest from the Sun.

In Roman mythology Neptune is known as the god of the sea called Poseidon.

It is the fourth largest planet in the solar system and smallest of the gas giants.

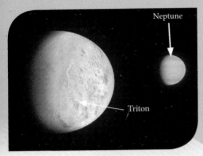

Triton, Proteus and Nereid are the three biggest Moons orbiting Neptune. Triton is almost as big as the Moon, and Nereid has a diameter of about 300 km. Proteus was discovered later.

**Neptune**

**Proteus**

Neptune has thirteen known moons. The largest, Triton, orbits Neptune in a direction opposite to the direction of the planet's rotation.

Triton's surface has many narrow valleys, craters and peaks, and frozen lakes of volcanic origin.

The Great Dark Spot is a hurricane-like storm on the planet that has been raging for at least 400 years.

The blue colour of the planet is due to the absorption of red light by methane in the atmosphere.

A large cloud named as "The Scooter" moves around Neptune every 16 hours.

Neptune's winds are the fastest in the solar system.

# Dwarf Planets

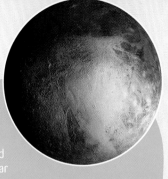

## PLUTO

Pluto is a small, icy "dwarf planet". Pluto's surface is said to be composed of a mixture of frozen nitrogen, methane and carbon monoxide ices. Pluto also has polar

**Charon**

**Pluto**

caps and regions of frozen methane and nitrogen. Pluto has not been visited by a spacecraft as yet. But in January 2006, NASA launched its New Horizons spacecraft to Pluto. It is expected to reach Pluto's surface by 2015.

Pluto has three known moons, Hydra, Nix, and Charon. It orbits in a disc-like zone beyond the orbit of Neptune called the *Kuiper belt*.

### Haumea

Haumea is the fourth largest dwarf planet located in the Kuiper belt. It is known to have two moons and to have a mass that is one-third of Pluto. It takes 285 Earth years for Haumea to make one orbit around the sun.

## ERIS

Eris (UB313) was named after the Greek goddess of discord and strife. Eris is also known as the icy dwarf planet. Eris is the most distant object ever seen in orbit around the Sun.

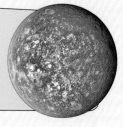

Eris is the largest dwarf planet in the Solar System with diameter between 2,400 and 3,000 kilometres.

## CERES

Ceres is named after the Roman goddess of the harvest. Ceres's shape resembles a flattened sphere with a diameter of about 590 miles (950 kilometres). It is made up of a rocky inner core surrounded by a mantle of water-ice. It was discovered by Italian astronomer Giuseppe Piazzi in 1801. Ceres has a very primitive surface and like a young planet, contains water-bearing minerals, and possibly a very weak atmosphere and frost. Ceres was initially classified as a comet but later it was categorised as a dwarf planet.

## MAKEMAKE

Makemake has been classified as a dwarf planet by the International Astronomical Union (IAU). Makemake is visually the second brightest *Kuiper belt* object after Pluto.

# Gallery of Moons

## JUPITER

Jupiter has sixteen moons

Four large Gallilean moons

**Io:** It is the fourth largest moon and the most volcanically active object in Solar System.

**Ganymede:** It is the largest of all Galilean moons and is the only moon known to have its own magnetic field.

Twelve small moons

Metis, Adrastea, Amalthea, Thebe, Elara, Ananke, Carme, Lysithea, Parsiphae, Sinope, Leda, Himalia

**Europa:** Its surface is composed of ice and is one of the smoothest in the Solar System.

**Callisto:** It is the third largest moon in the Solar System.

## MARS

Mars has two moons

Phobos

It is larger of the two moons. It is small and irregular shaped object and least reflective body in the Solar System.

Deimos

It is the outermost moon of Mars.

## EARTH

Earth has only one moon.

Dione

Titan

Rhea

Enceladus

## SATURN

Saturn has eighteen known moons. They are Titan, Rhea, Pan, Atlas, Mimas, Calypso, Dione, Lapetus, Hyperion, Janus, Phoebe, Enceladus, Dione, Telesto, Tethys, Promethus, Helene, Epimetheus

## URANUS

Uranus has twenty seven known moons. They are Titania, Oberon, Ariel, Umbriel, Miranda, Puck, Caliban, Sycorax, Prospero, Setebos, Stephano, Trinculo, Francisco, Ferdinand, Belinda, Cordelia, Ophelia, Desdemona, Bianca, Cressida, Juliet, Mab, Portia, Rosalind, Perdita, Cupid, Margaret.

Triton

Proteus

## NEPTUNE

Neptune has thirteen moons. They are Triton, Nereid, Halimede, Naiad, Thalassa, Despina, Galatea, Larissa, Proteus, Sao, Psamathe, Laomedeia, Neso

63

# SPACE EXPLORATION

In ancient times, humans were inseparably linked to the soil, but they still dreamed of flying. The sky was seen as a sphere that extended over the Earth and where the gods lived, but people still dreamed about going there. Their dreams became a reality beginning in the nineteenth century. It became possible to fly, and in the middle of the twentieth century, people succeeded in launching objects outside the planet. Those were the first attempts to make that old dream come true.

# Astronomy

Astronomy was long connected to astrology, which is devoted to interpreting human destiny by the stars. The first astronomers were priests who worked in the temples. The Greeks were the first ones who entirely separated astronomy and religion. That is when the history of astronomical science began.

*Galileo Gallilei studying the skies.*

*The Indian astronomical observatory of Jantar Mantar in Jaipur, India.*

*The Mayan pyramid El Adivino in Uxmal, Mexico.*

*Around 2,500 years ago the Greeks were the first to completely separate science from religion, thereby freeing up thought and making scientific advances possible.*

# Great Astronomers of Ancient Times

### Aristotle

This Greek philosopher was one of the main thinkers of ancient times and was dedicated to botany, zoology, psychology, medicine, physics, and astronomy, as well as philosophy.

Aristotle maintained that the Earth was a sphere that remained in a fixed position in space and was the center of the universe. The other planets, the stars, the Moon, and the Sun revolved around it.

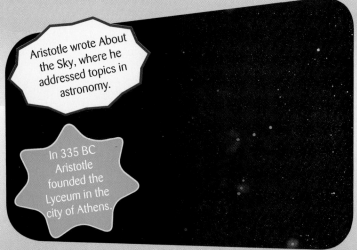

Aristotle wrote About the Sky, where he addressed topics in astronomy.

In 335 BC Aristotle founded the Lyceum in the city of Athens.

## Claudius Ptolemaeus (Ptolemy)

This Greek philosopher, mathematician, and astronomer assembled all the knowledge about astronomy that existed at that time. In addition, he created astronomical tables and he also made a catalogue that includes 1,200 stars.

His main contribution to this science is the planetary model he created and described in five books. His concept of the universe was adopted by astronomers and lasted for more than thirteen centuries.

## Ptolemy's Model of the Universe

The system proposed by Ptolemy considered that the Earth was the center of the universe. He maintained that the Earth was a sphere and that the Moon, the planets, the Sun, and the stars were arranged around it, revolving in precise orbits. In order to explain observed irregularities, Ptolemy invented a complicated set of corrective calculations.

# Modern Astronomers

The fifteenth century produced the first great revolution when Copernicus stated that the Earth was not the center of the universe. From that time onwards astronomy began its transformation into the science that we know today.

*Copernicus assembled his theory in a work that was opposed by the Church, but he saw it published during his lifetime.*

*Copernicus maintained that the Earth and the other planets revolved around the Sun*

## Nicholas Copernicus

A Polish astronomer, Copernicus devised some very useful inventions.

He was a careful analyst of all the theories known at that time, and he compared them with the most recent available information, and with his own observations. All this led him to conclude that the Earth was not the center of the universe.

# Galileo Galilei

This Italian mathematician, astronomer, and physicist constructed an improved telescope that magnified thirty times and that he used to study the stars.

He made some very important contributions to astronomy, such as the discovery of sunspots, calculating the rotational period of the Sun, and determining that the stars are very far from our planet, and that the universe may be infinite. He was a great defender of the theory of Copernicus which stated that the Earth was not the centre of the Universe.

Galileo demonstrated that the Milky Way is not a cloud but a large number of stars.

Other discoveries of Galileo include the mountains on the Moon and four of Jupiter's satellites.

According to legend, after renouncing the Copernican theory in front of the judges of the Inquisition, Galileo asserted that "in spite of that (the Earth) does move."

# Space Exploration

## The First Attempts

Since ancient times, humans have dreamed of flying. The dreams became a reality in the middle of the twentieth century, people succeeded in launching objects outside the planet. Those were the first attempts to make that old dream come true.

## Chinese Rockets

Fireworks are an ancient application of gunpowder. They involve launching a small rocket into the air so that it explodes at a certain altitude and sends out coloured sparks in all directions.

*A scene from the movie From the Earth to the Moon, based on the work by Jules Verne.*

## Jules Verne

This French writer was born in 1828 and died in 1905. He was the author of many adventure books such as Around the World in Eighty Days, A Journey to the Center of the Earth, and Twenty Thousand Leagues Under the Sea. In all his works he shows a great vision of the future accomplishments of science and technology.

## To Leave the Earth

Among many other calculations, Verne determined that the minimum speed required to escape the Earth's gravity is 6.83 miles (11.2 km) per second.

Jules Verne described the effects of weightlessness on space travellers.

## The Father of Astronautics

The Russian K. E. Tsiolkowski was the first scientist to dedicate himself to the basic problems of space travel. One basic idea he proposed was the use of liquid fuels instead of solid ones.

## Esnault-Pelterie

The Frenchman R. Esnault-Pelterie designed various propulsion motors and furthered the possibilities of using nuclear fuels.

The first rocket prototypes created by Tsiolkowski in 1914 and 1915.

## Von Braun

The German engineer Wernher von Braun constructed the famous V-2.

## Goddard

The American R. H. Goddard succeeded in launching a rocket using liquid oxygen and alcohol fuel, just as Tsiolkowski had proposed years before.

The deadly V-2 flying bombs were the precursors of present-day missiles; after the war they served as rockets at the start of the Space Race.

## Oberth

Another German, Hermann Oberth collaborated on the production of the V-2 and after that he continued his studies on spaceship propulsion in the United States.

## The Space Race

Once World War II was over, the old Allies, the United States and the Soviet Union and began special programs designed to reach the Moon. That became known as the Space Race.

The first step in the Space Race involved building rockets that were capable of overcoming the Earth's gravity.

The principle of the propulsion rocket. The oxidizing agent (1) makes it possible for the fuel to burn; the pump or gas impeller (2) pumps the fuel from the tank to the motor (3), where the fuel generates gas as it burns.

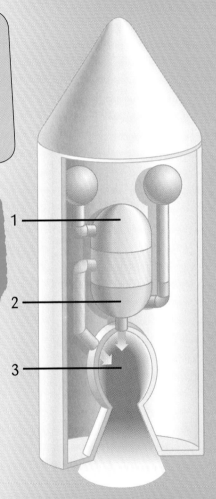

1

2

3

## The Starting Gun

The Space Race officially began on July 29, 1955. On that day, the United States announced that it would construct and launch into space an artificial satellite that would enter into orbit around the Earth and take photographs of our planet. On August 1, 1955, three days after the American announcement, the Soviets also announced their intention to build and put into orbit a similar satellite.

The gigantic rocket Saturn 5 (110 m high and 2,700 metric tons in weight) made it possible for humans to reach the Moon.

## How does a Rocket Work?

A simple rocket consists of a propulsion chamber where the liquid fuel is burned, and that expels gases at more than 5,000 degrees Fahrenheit. For that purpose, the turbines have to be very durable so they don't melt. The escaping gases propel the rocket in the opposite direction. The payload is located at the opposite end; that may be other rockets or a space capsule.

## The First Artificial Satellite

On October 4, 1957, Soviet scientists put into orbit the first artificial satellite to orbit around the Earth; it was named Sputnik I. Space exploration had begun. That first satellite was small, no bigger than a large ball; it was silver in colour and had several antennae.

Four months after Sputnik I was launched (in the illustration) the first American satellite, Explorer I, was put into orbit.

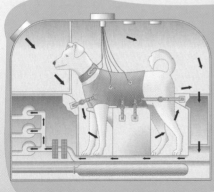

## The First Living Creature in Space

On November 3, 1957, the Russians put a new satellite into orbit; it was named Sputnik II, and it carried inside it a Siberian Husky named Laika, who became the first living being to leave the Earth and venture into space.

## Travelling Monkeys And Rats

While the Soviet scientists were using Siberian Huskies as astronauts, the Americans opted to use rats and monkeys. Flights involving monkeys were more successful; they provided valuable information subsequent manned flights.

NASA (the National Aeronautics and Space Administration) was formed in July, 1958; it is the American civilian organization that deals with all matters involving aeronautics.

## Men in Space

When construction techniques for rockets had reached a certain level that allowed launching a large capsule, and experiments with animals had demonstrated that it was possible to live in space, the two great national powers went a step farther, and for the first time humans succeeded in leaving the planet. A new age had begun.

### Yuri Gagarin

The pilot Yuri Gagarin, became the first person to travel into space, on April 12, 1961. He did so on board a small capsule named Vostok 1. His flight lasted just a few hours, during which he made one revolution around the Earth.

### John Glenn

John H. Glenn made a couple of trips around the Earth, and he remained in communication with ground control from his spaceship; these communications were broadcast to the public, and caused a major sensation.

## The Mercury Project

Many other launches, both Soviet and American, followed the first two manned flights into space. The capsules were tight quarters that had room for only one crew member. The American flights involving a single crew member were designated the Mercury project.

*A Mercury capsule after landing at sea.*

*An American space capsule landing in the ocean.*

*A Soviet space capsule landing in Siberia.*

## The Apollo Mission

After the success of the first manned space flights, NASA began the Apollo project at the end of 1966, with the ambitious plan of putting a man on the Moon. That was achieved three years later.

## Landing on the Moon

The Definitive Flight: On 16 July 1969, Apollo 11 balsted off from Cape Kennedy en route to the Moon. Three days later it entered the orbit of the Moon.

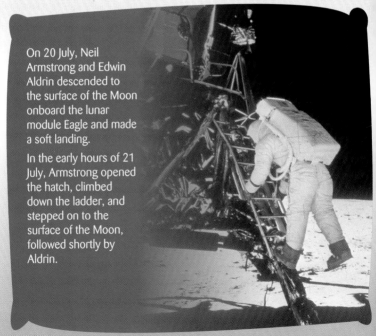

On 20 July, Neil Armstrong and Edwin Aldrin descended to the surface of the Moon onboard the lunar module Eagle and made a soft landing.

In the early hours of 21 July, Armstrong opened the hatch, climbed down the ladder, and stepped on to the surface of the Moon, followed shortly by Aldrin.

## A Historic Step

When Neil Armstrong climbed down the ladder of the lunar module and steeped onto the ground, the module's television cameras captured the moment and transmitted it to the Earth, where hundreds of millions of spectators were able to follow the event directly. The astronauts were moving around and were able to jump effortlessly due to the reduced gravitational force.

Neil Armstrong said these famous words on television: "That's one small step for [a] man, one giant leap for mankind."

There have been six other manned expeditions to the Moon (Apollo 12 to Apollo 17) since the first landing.

## Space Exploration beyond the Moon

In the 1960s the conquest of the Moon was one of the most important programmes carried out by NASA and by Soviet scientists. But at the same time there were other projects of greater scope and duration that targeted longer-term results: space exploration beyond the Moon.

## Conquering the Planets

Between the years 1962 and 1973 both space powers launched numerous satellites headed for the main planets of the Solar System; they obtained closer photographs and some data about their surface. In the subsequent years it has finally been possible to use the photos in drawing up maps of those planets, and to touch down on some of them.

Life on Mars?: In 1970 the Russian spacecraft Venera 7 landed successfully on the surface of Venus, and other spaceships in this series repeated the feat in the following years. The American spacecraft Viking I and Viking II arrived on Mars in 1976 and carried out experiments to search for signs of life, but they found none.

Probing Venus: In 1978 Pioneer Venus 2 launched several probes on parachutes onto the surface of Venus.

And Beyond…: Voyager I and II were launched in 1977. They passed close to Jupiter in 1979; Saturn in 1980 and 1981; Uranus in 1986; and Neptune in 1989.

In 1997 Mars Pathfinder deposited a vehicle onto the surface of Mars.

# EARTH

Of all the planets that make up the Solar System, the Earth is the only one that supports life. Astronauts have always described the Earth as a blue planet because of the oceans and the gasses that surround it. The coverings of water, land and air are unique in the whole Solar System and are the main components that make life possible.

# Earth

Our planet Earth, together with other planets, satellites and smaller bodies, forms part of the Solar System.

The Earth differs from the rest of the planets in three important ways. First, it has water in liquid form which covers most of its surface. Earth's atmosphere is mostly oxygen. Most importantly, there is life on Earth. Up to now, no form of life has been found anywhere else in the Solar System.

## The Future of the Earth

At present, Earth is a planet which has the right conditions for developing and sustaining life. We are not sure that these conditions will continue for many more years. Human activity can change the conditions on earth forever.

## Climate Change

Factories and industries release huge amounts of carbon dioxide, which has steadily led to the phenomenon known as the greenhouse effect, where the temperature of the Earth increases, just like inside a greenhouse. This happens because the incoming solar radiation after striking the Earth is absorbed by atmospheric carbon dioxide and is not entirely reflected back into space. Although, this prevents the Earth from freezing and keeps all life processes going, heat build-up beyond a certain point can have very harmful effects.

Several international treaties have been signed to limit the emission of greenhouse gases and prevent climate change.

Carbon dioxide emission may be restricted by switching over from fossil fuels to non-conventional forms of energy. The advantage of using non-conventional energy resources like nuclear, solar, wind, or tidal energy and bio-fuels is that they are inexhaustible (unlike carbon-based fuels) and greatly reduce air pollution and prevent global warming. Recycling of used products also significantly helps in this process.

## Biodiversity

Biodiversity refers to the variation in the life forms at the levels of genes, species and ecosystems. This is essential for the harmonious coexistence of plant and animals on the Earth. Man-made phenomena are responsible for the loss of biodiversity and the extinction of many species across the world. It is very important to reverse this process as biodiversity not only sustains but also enriches human life. For instance, the existence of a wide variety of plant species not only assists in agriculture (resulting in increased food production) but also helps in the discovery of many new medicines. Several ecosystems like mangroves and coral reefs not only provide shelter to varied life forms, but also help us at times of distress.

87

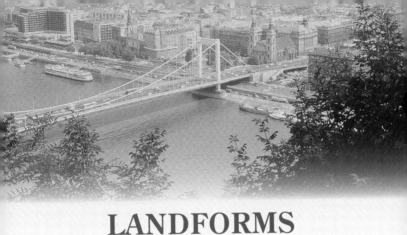

# LANDFORMS

The shape of the land depends mostly on the rock that lies beneath it. Over millions of years, natural processes have shaped the rock into what we say today: mountains or valleys, plains or hills, cliffs or sandy beaches.

# The Shape of the Land

Mountains and lakes, rolling hills, flat plains, and rocky outcrops are features of a landscape that is always changing.

The earth's surface is cracked into plates, which float on a layer of semi-molten rock. Forces in this layer cause the plates to move. In some places, they collide; in others, they move apart. Where they collide, the land may buckle up into mountains, called fold mountains.

The shape of the land is created by forces within the earth, but is continually changed by the actions of weathering, water, and other natural agents on the surface.

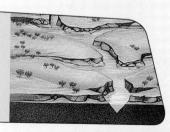

As fast as mountains form, they begin to be broken down by natural forces. Rain, wind, frost, and ice carve the rocky surface into a variety of shapes, and over millions of years, these forces wear it flat.

Earth's movements create mountains, rivers carve valleys, and rocks are worn down and carried to the sea.

Rivers carve valleys and carry the broken rock particles, called sediment, to the sea. The sediment settles in layers on the seabed. In time, sediment forms new rock that may later be raised up by the earth's movements.

# Erosion

The earth's surface is constantly under attack. It is worn away, or eroded, by weathering—extremes of temperature and chemical action—and the forces of wind, water, and ice.

On seacoasts, waves carrying sand and pebbles endlessly pound the shore. They cut into a cliff face and weaken its base. Eventually, the rock, soil, and vegetation on top collapse and leave a bare cliff.

On land, the wind acts like a sandblaster. It picks up dust and sand and hurls it at rocks. Because the wind cannot lift the particles high, the rock is worn down more at ground level than higher up. This results in irregularly shaped formations.

On high mountains, the snow never melts. It builds up in layers many feet deep. The fresh snow weighs down on the snow underneath and compacts it into ice. As the ice thickens, it becomes heavier and begins to move downhill under its own weight. It becomes a river of ice called a glacier.

The scenery in many desert regions results from ancient glaciers and rivers.

## The Abundant Rain Forests

Nowhere on earth is plant and animal life as abundant as in tropical rain forests. The plants grow close together because the water and warmth they need is available all year.

Plant life in tropical rain forests is more diverse than anywhere else on earth.

The diversity of animal life in rain forests is as rich as that of the plants.

## The Savannas, Home of the Herds

Savannas are tropical grasslands with widely scattered trees and shrubs. They are the home of elephants and herds of other grazing animals that feed on clumps of grass and gather at water holes.

Savanna grass has thick blades that conserve moisture. There is too little water for most trees to grow, but acacia and baobab trees have ways to survive drought.

Every year, when the long dry season ends, huge fires sweep across the African savannas. Burning gives new life to the savanna. The ashes of the burned grass enrich the soil and help new grass to grow. Different animals graze the new grass in succession.

## Survival in the Desert

Hot deserts have an almost unbearable climate. Temperatures may rise to more than 100°F (38°C) by day and drop to the freezing point at night. Water is scarce or nonexistent.

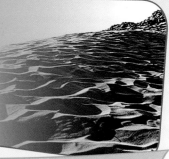

Life still manages to survive because both animals and plants have adapted to these conditions.

An oasis is a green and fertile place in the desert, where there is always enough water to keep plants and animals alive. The water comes from springs, underground streams, or wells.

## Grasslands

The prairies, the pampas of South America, the veld of southern Africa, and the steppes of Eurasia are the great temperate grasslands of the world. Like the savannas, they have a long dry season that restricts tree growth.

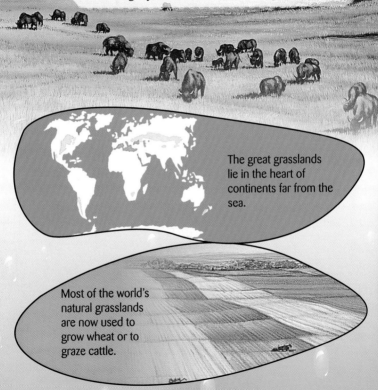

The great grasslands lie in the heart of continents far from the sea.

Most of the world's natural grasslands are now used to grow wheat or to graze cattle.

## The Northern Forests

Most of the world's temperate forests are in the northern hemisphere. Thousands of years ago, Europe was nearly one vast forest, as was much of northern North America and Asia. As soon as human beings developed tools, they began to cut down trees for firewood, timber, and farmland. Even so, much natural forest still remains.

The types of trees that grow vary with the climate. In the north are evergreen coniferous trees that can withstand long, bitter winters. To the south are broad-leaved deciduous trees that shed their leaves once a year.

In Mediterranean woodlands, the trees are mostly evergreens, with small tough leaves that can cope with strong summer sunlight and a shortage of water.

Many animals make their homes in undisturbed areas of the forest.

## Life in the Tundra

The tundra is a region of treeless plains in far northern North America, Europe, and Asia. For most of the year, the temperature stays below the freezing point. During the long, dark winter, icy winds blow and snow covers the ground. Summers are short and cool, but there is enough sunlight and heat for a carpet of low-growing plants to burst into flower and make their seeds.

## Marshes, Swamps, and Mangroves

Bog, marsh, swamp, and fen are some of the names given to wet, spongy land where the water level remains near or above the surface.

Wetlands are found all over the world. Many of them are protected habitats, but others are in danger from developers who drain the land and build on it.

Wetlands are a refuge for many animals, including the saltwater crocodile. Instead of being drained, many marshes are now being conserved.

99

Landforms are natural shapes or features of the earth. They are defined by their surface form and location in the landscape. The physical features that dominate the landscape such as mountains, plains and valleys, strike us as external and unchangeable, and most of the time, we are not able to observe changes of any importance. Just the same, these features are in continual transformation.

## The Formation of Mountains

Even though mountains appear huge to us, when they are viewed from outer space, or even from an airplane, they appear to be a small alteration in the relief of the Earth's crust. However, they are extremely important for the life of all organisms. Mountains are the result of the Earth's crust folding and rising in elevation in certain areas.

## The Age of Mountains

When you travel, you encounter many types of mountains. Some have a high, pointed peak, and others have a rounded or flat summit. The former are more recent because they have not yet been subjected to erosion, which removes material over the course of millions of years and smoothes out shapes as if they had been "filed down," which is what has happened to old mountains.

Between the mountains we find valleys. A valley is a lowland area that slopes down to a stream, lake or the ocean, formed by water or ice erosion.

A plateau is a flat area, higher than the area around it. Like all elevated regions, plateaus were caused by years of erosion and still are. Low plateaus are used as farming regions and high one are used for livestock grazing. However, most of the world's high plateaus are desert areas.

A cave is an underground hollow or passage which is formed by erosion by water flowing underground. When rainwater seeps into the soil it mixes with the gases produced by the decayed plant material in the soil. This produces what is commonly knows as ground water. Limestone is a rock that is soluble in water. The ground water dissolves the limestone, thereby creating a cave. This of course is a really lengthy process. It can take millions of years for a cave to be formed.

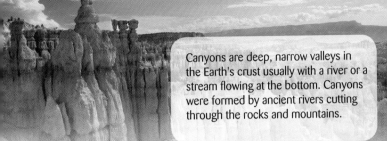

Canyons are deep, narrow valleys in the Earth's crust usually with a river or a stream flowing at the bottom. Canyons were formed by ancient rivers cutting through the rocks and mountains.

Islands can be defined as pieces of solid ground surrounded by water. They are differentiated from continents, which also appear to be surrounded by water on all sides, by their size because they are considerably smaller. They may be volcanic or coral in origin, prolongations of a continent, or the exposed tops of underwater mountains, but one characteristic they all have is that they have a climate that is strongly influenced by the ocean, as we would expect.

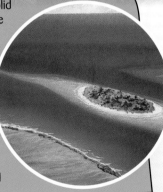

## Archipelagos

Archipelagos are made up of several islands with similar characteristics that constitute a geographic unit.

Very small islands are known as islets.

# Water & Oceans

If the oceans were drained, the ocean floor would have the same appearance as land. It is rough and uneven, with mountain ridges and deep trenches.

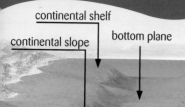

continental shelf

continental slope

bottom plane

deep sea trench

People once thought that the ocean floor was a vast, flat plain. But scientists have discovered that it is as varied as land areas, with plains, mountain ranges, huge volcanoes, canyons, and even deeper trenches.

## Water and the Ocean Floor

The Terrain under the Sea: The four typical areas that make up the terrain beneath the sea are

- continental shelf: a plain of variable width that borders the continents and extends to a depth of 200 m and this where most underwater life exists;

- continental slope: a fairly pronounced slope that goes down to a depth of about 2,500-3,500 m;

- bottom plane: constitutes the ocean floor at a depth of about of about 3,500 m-6,000 m and contains numerous mountains chains called undersea ridges and trenches;

- deep sea trenches: with depths that can exceed 10,000 m.

Earth contains three large ocean basins and one smaller basin. They are the Pacific Ocean, which is the largest and covers about a third of the earth's surface; the Atlantic Ocean; the Indian Ocean; and the Arctic Ocean. All these oceans are interconnected.

Linked to the oceans are smaller areas called seas.

## The Pacific

The Pacific is the largest ocean on the planet; it stretches from Asia to the American continent.

The bottom of the Pacific exhibits great volcanic activity. It is also the ocean with the greatest average depth and the one with the greatest maximum depth.

## The Indian Ocean

The Indian Ocean is the third largest ocean based on surface area and spans between the eastern shores of Africa, southern Asia, Australia, and Antarctica.

## The Atlantic

The second largest ocean, the Atlantic stretches between Europe and Africa in its eastern reaches, and to America in its western.

The main regional seas are the Mediterranean Sea, the North Sea, the Baltic Sea and the Caribbean Sea

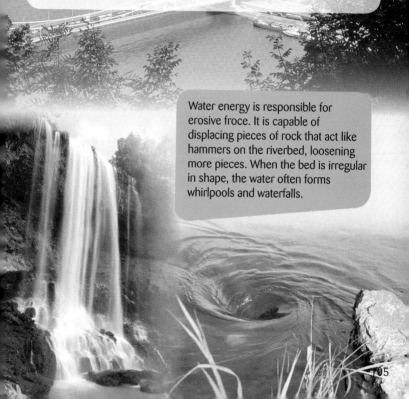

# Rivers

Even though they account for only a small amount of all the water on the planet, the waters that run on the surface of exposed land are very important for all living creatures, both plants and animals. They generally are the direct result of precipitation that falls as rain, snow, and hail and the large deposits (aquifers) that this water forms; as a result of the force of gravity, many of them end up emptying into the oceans.

Water energy is responsible for erosive froce. It is capable of displacing pieces of rock that act like hammers on the riverbed, loosening more pieces. When the bed is irregular in shape, the water often forms whirlpools and waterfalls.

## Underground Waters

Underground water comes from rain. It forms large deposits, which in many areas are the only source of potable water. When these waters flow beneath the ground, they sometimes carve out great systems of caves and galleries.

Geysers: At times the underground water reaches deeper layers or areas where there is volcanic activity, is heated, and comes to the surface in a fountain that can shoot up dozens of yards in the form of a geyser.

Springs and Wells: A spring is a natural water outlet on the surface of the ground when the mantle is free. Springs commonly form because the impermeable layer lies on a slope that intersects with the surface at the point where the spring appears.

A well is an artificial outlet made in captive mantle, allowing the water to come out under high pressure whenever the well is located below the highest level of the mantle. If the perforation is located at a point higher than the mantle, the water needs to be extracted by pumps.

## Lakes

Sometimes lakes are considered miniature seas, and there are some similarities. They are masses of fresh or brackish water found inland on continents or islands and generally are connected to a river system. Some lakes are an important water supply for settlements near the shore, and they are crucial to fauna.

The depression or cavity that contains a lake's water is called a basin.

A pond is smaller than a lake, and the body of water is always a homogeneous mix.

## Glaciers

The huge masses of ice that cover the poles and high areas of the world's major mountain chains are called glaciers. They are the remains of the ice covering that once extended over a large part of the upper latitudes of the planet in the course of the last glaciations. Glaciers play an extremely important role in the process of erosion.

107

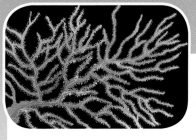

## Coral Reefs

The delicate tangled twigs (right) look like the branches of plants sculpted in stone. They are not plants, however, but living organisms, called corals. Corals are mostly colonial animals that live in tropical seas.

Millions of them live together and their abandoned skeletons build up into huge structures, called reefs or coral islands (below).

When a coral reproduces, the young coral remains attached to its parent, and so the colony grows.

Coral reefs (top) are the home of great numbers of brightly colored fish, crustaceans, mollusks, sea anemones, starfish, and worms. Because reefs provide animals with protection and places to hide, they are major breeding grounds.

Although coral reefs are hard, they are also fragile. Pollutants from factories and agriculture can easily destroy living colonies.

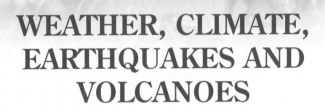

# WEATHER, CLIMATE, EARTHQUAKES AND VOLCANOES

Mountains and lakes, rolling hills, flat plains, and rocky outcrops are features of a landscape that is always changing by the actions of many natural processes like weather, climate, earthquakes and volcanoes.

# Weather and Climate

## What is Weather?

Weather is the condition of the sky and the air outside. Rain, wind, air, energy from the Sun, moisture in the air and cloud cover all together create our weather. Weather can change often in short periods. This is because of the winds and storms prevailing at a particular time. Weather only happens at the lowest layer of the atmosphere closest to the surface of the Earth which is called the troposphere.

### Did you know?

Weather has caused more deaths than any other natural force on the planet.

## What is Climate?

Climate is the pattern of weather over a long period in a particular region. It is the average weather of a region and includes all weather conditions like the four weather seasons—winter, spring, summer and autumn and weather disasters like tornadoes, storms, floods, etc. and is usually taken over a 30 year time period.

## Can you differentiate between Weather and Climate?

Climate is not the same as weather, but is the average pattern of weather for a particular region. Weather describes the short-term state of the atmosphere whereas climate gives the total description of all weather over a longer span of time.

# Seasons

**Did you know?**

There are no seasons in the grasslands of Savannah and hence the climate is determined by a rainy season in summer and a dry spell in winter.

## Why do we have Seasons?

Since the Earth is round, the Sun does not heat the Earth evenly. The sun is almost directly overhead at the equator so the heat is intense. Farther away from the equator, the heat is less strong. This is why it is always cold at the poles.

As the earth spins on its axis, it also travels around the Sun taking a year to complete each round. The earth does not spin upright; it tilts on its axis. This tilt points one side of the earth toward the sun and then the other. Therefore, the parts of the earth that lean toward the sun receive more light and heat than the parts tilted away from it. This is the cause of the existence of seasons. In regions that lean toward the sun, it is summer. In regions tilted away from the sun, it is winter and in between these seasons are spring or autumn.

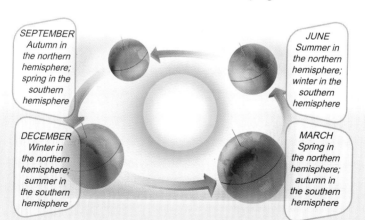

SEPTEMBER
Autumn in the northern hemisphere; spring in the southern hemisphere

JUNE
Summer in the northern hemisphere; winter in the southern hemisphere

DECEMBER
Winter in the northern hemisphere; summer in the southern hemisphere

MARCH
Spring in the northern hemisphere; autumn in the southern hemisphere

113

The atmosphere is the blanket of air that surrounds the Earth. It shields the Earth from the harmful rays of the sun and helps to keep it warm. The lowest layer of the atmosphere, called the troposphere is where all the weather phenomena take place.

Weather is a combination of three elements in the atmosphere. They are humidity, temperature and atmospheric pressure.

Temperature is the degree of hotness or coldness in a particular region, atmospheric pressure is the amount of force exerted on you by the weight of the air and humidity is the amount of invisible gas, called water vapour, present in the air. Together, these three elements bring about the formation of winds, clouds, rain, snow, fog, dust storms, etc, as well as the less frequent phenomena like tornadoes, typhoons, ice storms, hurricanes, lightning, blizzards and many more.

## Humidity

The more water vapour there is in the air, the higher is the humidity. Water evaporates and rises into the sky where it turns into water droplets and forms clouds. The water droplets join together to make larger drops that fall to the earth as rain.

Humidity is measured by two kinds of instruments – they are the hygrometer and the psychrometer.

## Temperature

The average temperature of any place in the world depends on the amount of the sun's heat it receives – the lesser heat a region receives, the colder it is. Regions along the equator receive more heat and farthest at the poles, the regions are extremely cold.

The temperature of a region not only depends on its closeness to the equator but also its height and nearness to the sea. Mountain areas are therefore cooler than lowland areas.

The instrument used to measure temperature is called a thermometer.

## Atmospheric pressure

Atmospheric pressure makes the wind blow thereby affecting the weather. Warm air is lighter than cold air so the warm rises and the cold air comes down to replace it. When this happens, the wind moves from areas where it is colder to areas where it is warmer. The shorter the distance between the high and low pressure areas, the faster the wind blows. The instrument used to measure atmospheric pressure or as it is more commonly known, air pressure, is a barometer.

# Clouds

## Clouds

A cloud is a great mass of billions of tiny water droplets or ice crystals. These water droplets are so light that they float in the air.

### What are Clouds made up of?

Clouds are formed when air is cooled below its saturation point. When air passes over a warm land surface, it heats up and rises. As it rises, it cools and forms clouds. Air must rise when it blows over mountains, and this makes it form clouds. Lighter warm air rides up over heavier cold air.

## Types of Clouds

Clouds often change their shape when they evaporate or condense. Some are white and fluffy, others are dark and menacing.

Cirrostratus clouds are thin sheets of ice crystals that look like a veil.

Cirrus clouds look like wispy streaks of white hair, sometimes called mares' tails.

Cirrocumulus is caused by strong winds at very high altitudes. It usually appears in small patches that may look like fish scales.

Cumulonimbus are towering anvil-shaped thunderclouds that pile up high in the sky and discharge rain, hail, and lightning.

Altostratus clouds consist of water droplets. They form a smooth gray sheet of cloud and causes drizzle rather than rain.

Altocumulus is made of water droplets, it appears as layers of puffy white or gray clouds that signal a change in the weather.

Stratus is the lowest kind of cloud. It forms a low, gray sheet. At ground level, stratus clouds form fog.

Cumulus are white puffy clouds that often float in the sky on sunny days.

Nimbostratus is a sheet of grey cloud that produces continuous rain or snow.

Stratocumulus clouds form in pale or dark layers and often extend over thousands of square miles. They create an overcast sky but rarely give rain.

# Precipitation

After water evaporates to the air to form clouds, a process called condensation occurs. This is when the water vapour which has turned to gas changes its form to liquid.

## RAIN CYCLE

When clouds become too heavy, a process in which water vapour in the air changes its form to liquid takes place. This process is called condensation. When water droplets fall back to the surface of the earth, this phenomenon is called precipitation. Precipitation always comes from clouds. This process is known as the rain cycle.

### Rain

Rain refers to the drops of fresh water that fall as precipitation from clouds. It is a form of precipitation in which water falls back to earth as a liquid rather than solid.

Rainfall is measured by an instrument called the rain gauge. When it rains, the rainfall goes into the rain gauge. The depth of the water inside it is used to measure the rainfall.

## Snow

Snow is frozen water. It is the precipitation falling from clouds in the form of ice crystals. It is made up of tiny, six-sided ice crystals, which form on dust particles inside very cold clouds. The crystals grow in size and join together. They become heavy and drop down through the clouds.

## Why do we have Snowfall??

When the temperature in a cloud drops far below the freezing point, ice crystals are formed inside it. As ice crystals form, they collide with each other, become heavier and drop down on earth in the form of patterned snowflakes.

**Did you know?**
No two snowflake shapes are ever alike.

## Drizzle

Drizzle is light rain precipitation consisting of liquid water drops smaller than those of rain, and generally smaller than 0.5 mm (0.02 in.) in diameter.

## Sleet

Sleet is partially melted snow. Sleet forms when a raindrop or a snowflake partially melts as it falls through a layer of warm air higher in the atmosphere and turns back into ice as it falls through a deep layer of cold air at the surface.

## Ice Pellets

Ice pellets refers to the precipitation that comes in the form of transparent ice. They can come in the form of either frozen raindrops or snow pellets, covered by a thin layer of ice which resulted from partial melting and became frozen again.

## Graupel

Graupel is a type of snow that falls not as snowflakes but as hard ice pellets. Graupel is usually the size of a coin and can be confused with hail. The difference between the two is the fact that hail is hard and graupel is softer and typically falls apart when touched or when it falls to the ground.

### Freezing Rain

Freezing rain is rain which falls while temperatures are just below the freezing point. Freezing rain is formed when warm air and cold air combine causing the rain to fall and freeze at the same time.

## Frost

When the air temperature drops below freezing point, the water vapour in the air freezes into ice crystals called frost. Frost forms on surfaces like on leaves of plants, cars, etc.

## Fog

Fog, like the clouds is formed by millions of little droplets of water that float in the air. While clouds rise up high in the skies, fog falls closer to the surface of the earth.

## Hailstones

Hailstones are a form of precipitation where chunks of ice or irregular balls of ice fall from the sky.

**Did you know?**
The largest hailstone ever recorded fell on 22nd June 2003 in south-central Nebraska, and measured 17 cm in diameter and 45 cm in circumference.

When ice crystals begin to fall towards the Earth, the wind blows and pushed them back up to the clouds. When they begin to fall down again, they keep growing in size, collecting more and more ice crystals from the clouds. Just as they come closer to the Earth's surface, they get blown up once again. This continues till the ice crystals become so large and heavy that the wind can no longer push them up. They fall on Earth as huge, solid rocks of ice called hailstones. Their size of course, can differ from the size of a small marble to that of a baseball.

123

## Frostbite

Frostbite happens due to the excessive exposure to extremely cold weather. It usually affects the toes, fingers, ears, and the tip of the nose. Frostbite can be very dangerous as there is no sensation of pain, and the victim may not even know that they have been frostbitten.

## Flood

Floods arise out of excess rainfall or melting snow in a particular area when rivers rise and the water goes over the banks. When there is a flood, the roads are full of water; sometimes, the water even goes inside people's homes!

### Quick Note

The Earth has a limited amount of water. Water keeps going around and around in a cycle, in the form of oceans, clouds, water vapour and precipitation so it keeps using that same water over and over again. Do you know what that means? It means that rain water is as old as our planet – which is more than 4 billion years old!

# Spectacular Sky Displays

## Rainbow

Rainbows occur when sunlight is seen through raindrops. The raindrops break up the sun's white light and reflect it back to an observer as seven different colours – red, orange, yellow, green, blue, indigo and violet – the colours of the rainbow.

You can only see a rainbow when you stand with your back to the sun. Large raindrops produce the best rainbows. Sometimes, you may be lucky enough to see a double rainbow.

## Fogbow

A fog bow is a white arc which appears in fog. Like a rainbow, a fogbow is caused when sunlight is seen through water droplets. Yet, the water droplets through which the sunlight passes in a fog bow are really small as compared to those of a rainbow. Hence, because of these tiny water droplets, the fogbow produces very faint colours and thus appears more like a white bow. A fog bow has sometimes been called a cloud bow.

## Halo

Like both the rainbow and the fog bow, the halo or also called the icebow also gets its light from the sun. Yet, this light does not pass through water droplets. Instead, it passes through ice crystals in the clouds. The only time that this can be seen is when the sun is high up in the horizon.

## Moonbow

Unlike the rainbow, the fog bow and the Icebow, the Moonbow does not take its light from the sun. Rather, it is produced by light reflected from the moon. It is fainter than the others and is visible always on the opposite part of the sky from the moon.

# Wind and Wind Patterns

Wind is simply air in motion. As we have already mentioned, warm air is light, so it rises thereby making way for the cold air to move in. This movement of air makes the wind blow.

### The Wind and our Environment

- The wind helps the growth of plants and trees by scattering their seeds all around.

- It helps to dry clothes; it turns the windmills and even pushes the sailboats through the water.

- The wind can be used to create electricity through wind power.

- If there was no wind, we wouldn't be able to fly kites

### Did you know?

The ancient Greeks thought that the wind was simply the Earth breathing in and out.

Wind appears in many forms, some are pleasant and useful and others are dangerous and destructive.

**Strong Wind**

**Light Breeze**

# Wind

**Storm**

**Hurricane**

## Did you know?

Without the wind, Columbus would never have been able to sail his ship and discover America.

## Wind Patterns

Different parts of the Earth receive different amounts of heat. Near the equator, the Sun is overhead and heats the Earth intensely. Near the poles, the sun's rays strike the earth at a low angle and so the heat is not so intense.

There is a general pattern of air circulation around the world. Although these winds are not constant, they blow more often than any other wind in the same area. This is why they are called prevailing winds.

Their direction is affected by the earth's rotation and by local conditions.

129

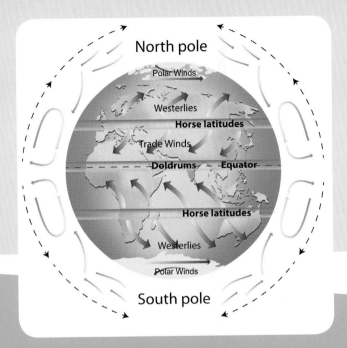

Rising air at the equator causes calm conditions known as the doldrums.

Immediately to the north of the doldrums as well as its south, is a zone where steady northeast winds blow. These are called the trade winds, because merchant ships that had sails took advantage of them.

Farther north in the northern hemisphere and south in the southern hemisphere is a band of prevailing westerlies.

Beyond it are the bitter polar winds sending strong winds toward the equator.

## Land Breeze

A Land Breeze occurs at night where the process is reversed. Cool air moves in from the land replacing the warm air above the surface of water.

## Sea Breeze

When the air above the land surface gets heated up by the sun, it rises up. Cool air from above the surface of the sea moves in to replace the warm air, cooling the land around it.

### Did you know?

Land and sea breezes can be seasonal also. They are called the monsoons and are responsible for bringing heavy rains. These are abundant in the tropical coastal countries of the Indian Ocean.

# Weather Phenomena

Hurricanes and tornadoes are the deadliest storms on the earth as these are powerful swirling masses of cyclonic wind, clouds and rain. They can wash away entire beaches, sink boats, pull trees right out of the ground and kill people.

## Thunderstorm

A thunderstorm is a violent storm that is accompanied by thunder, lightning, rain and sometimes hail. It is said that there are 40,000 thunderstorms taking place every day in different parts of the world. Thunderstorms can last up to an hour. Thunderstorms that do not produce rain are called dry thunderstorms and many a time, have been the cause of wildfires.

A thunderstorm begins when the wind picks up a lot of water creating cumulus clouds. In time, the water inside the cloud freezes into tiny particles of ice and later re-evaporates taking the form of cumulonimbus clouds. During a thunderstorm, the sky appears black or dark green. Severe thunderstorms can even rotate and have been the cause of many deaths and accidents.

Cumulonimbus cloud

**Did you know?**
The fear of lightning and thunder is called ASTRAPHOBIA.

## What is Lightning?

When liquid and ice particles above the freezing level collide and build up large electrical fields in the clouds, lightning is produced. It usually occurs during the thunderstorms.

## Tornado

A tornado is a small, but extremely disastrous whirlwind. It is the violent spinning air column connecting the thunderstorm to the ground. When warm air rises upwards in the form of a spiral below a powerful thunderstorm cloud, it gains the spinning speed and rises upwards. They can move at really fast speeds and can destroy everything in their path.

**Did you know?**

In 1931 a tornado in Mississippi lifted an 75 kg train and tossed it 24m from the track.

## What is a Gustnado?

A gustnado is a small and weak tornado that occurs along the gust front of a thunderstorm. They can do minor damage and are sometimes wrongly reported as tornadoes.

## Quck Facts

- Tornadoes can reach a wind speed of 500 kmph and hence can be very dangerous.
- Three out of every four tornadoes in the world occur in the United States.
- A tornado in Oklahoma on May 3, 1999 was the most destructive tornado in history causing over $1 billion in damage.
- Fujita Scale - The scale that measures the strength of tornadoes based upon the wind speed.

### Hurricane

Hurricanes are the deadliest storms on the earth as these are powerful swirling masses of cyclonic wind, clouds and rain. Tropical whirlwinds or cyclones are referred to as hurricanes. Hurricanes are characterized by a low-pressure core capable of generating thunderstorms. They can wash away entire beaches, sink boats, pull trees right out of the ground and kill people.

### What gives rise to the formation of a hurricane?

Hurricanes usually appear above the tropical waters when the temperatures are slightly high. This causes the enormous water to evaporate above the heated oceans. The water vapour starts rising up. The heat is released as moist air rises, during evaporation. Thus the condensation of water vapor fuels the formation of cyclonic windstorm.

135

## The Eye

The center of a hurricane is called the "eye" and it can be up to 20 miles across. Surprisingly, the weather in the "eye" is calm with low winds and clear skies.

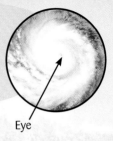

Eye

## Quick Facts

- The costliest hurricane of all time was Hurricane Andrew. Andrew struck Florida in 1992. The estimated cost damage was $26.5 billion.

- These whirlwinds are referred as 'hurricanes' in America, 'typhoons' in West Pacific, 'cyclones' in Indian ocean, and 'willy-willy' in Australia.

- The world's worst hurricane that caused the highest loss of life took place in Bangladesh in the year 1970. The hurricane created a flood that killed more than one million people.

- The intensity of a hurricane is measured on the Saffir-Simpson Scale.

### Waterspout

Waterspouts are most common over tropical or subtropical waters. They are similar in nature to of a tornado or a whirlwind, that appears above the ocean and larger water bodies. It has a funnel-like appearance. When this touches the surface of the water, water is pulled upwards inside the whirl. They sometimes rise up to a height of 450 metres in the sky.

## Blizzard

A blizzard is a kind of snowstorm but accompanied with winds blowing at a minimum speed of 35 miles per hour. A blizzard can be very dangerous as it reduces the visibility and thus bringing everything to a standstill.

## Supercell

A supercell thunderstorm includes a giant rotating updraft capable of producing tornadoes. Supercells are the strongest of all thunderstorms. In fact supercells are so large they show up on a satellite photograph in the shape of a tear drop. Most of the large tornadoes and giant hail events are spawned by supercells. The reason why supercells are the most severe is because of their rotating structure.

## Downburst

A downburst can be defined as the severe localized downward gust of air that can be experienced beneath a severe thunderstorm. These are the strong winds which move downward in a thunderstorm.

### Did you know?

A doppler radar is used to look inside thunderstorms where the movement of air can be seen.

On the 4th of July, 1977, a very strong and widespread downburst event hit northern Wisconsin with winds that were estimated to exceed 115 mph, which completely flattened thousands of acres of forest.

## Tsunami

It may be defined as the strong continuous water waves caused by the displacement of a large valume of a water body due to the factors like earthquake, volcanic eruption, etc.

## Sandstorm

Sandstrom are the strong winds that blow across the deserts and raises along large amout of sand, and thus reducing the visibility.

# Ocean Currents

Ocean currents involve the movement of great masses of water inside the ocean and seas due to the differences in pressure, temperature, and salinity that exist in different areas, as well as the constant action of the winds. In the latter case there established, representative currents in various parts of the globe. The Coriolis effect caused by the Earth's rotation, which affects the direction of the winds also has an influence on the ocean currents. These currents are extremely important to ocean life because they distribute the necessary nutrients for the growth of phytoplankton.

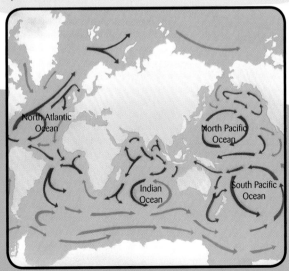

## Ocean Circulation

The great ocean currents are not a single mass of water, but rather are made up of many unified branches that contribute to the general movement. At first they join in two large circuits – the polar and the tropical – which distribute the waters in each hemisphere. But the continents cause these circuits to divide into smaller ones.

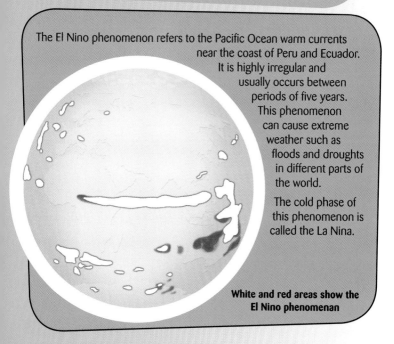

The El Nino phenomenon refers to the Pacific Ocean warm currents near the coast of Peru and Ecuador. It is highly irregular and usually occurs between periods of five years. This phenomenon can cause extreme weather such as floods and droughts in different parts of the world.

The cold phase of this phenomenon is called the La Nina.

**White and red areas show the El Nino phenomenan**

# Weather and Climate Forecasting

Scientists who study weather and climate are called meteorologists. They use different instruments like the wind vane, thermometer, anemometer, rain gauge, barometer, etc to keep track of the temperature of the air, the direction and speed of the wind, the change in air pressure, moisture in the air, the clouds and the amount of rainfall.

Satellites and sophisticated modern computers have revolutionized weather forecasting. Satellites in stationary or variable orbits provide pictures of weather worldwide. Further contributions come from weather ships, weather observatories, and balloon-borne equipment. Meteorologists translate the computer results into weather forecasts for aircraft, ships, and farmers; into reports for radio and television; into maps for newspapers; and into temperature forecasts.

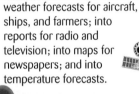

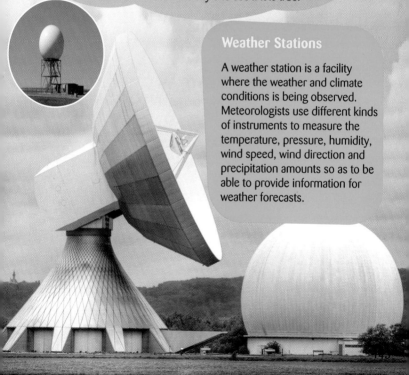

## Did you know?

Long ago, people looked for clues in nature to predict the weather. The sound of frogs croaking loudly was a sign of rain on the way. Closed pinecones meant wet weather; open ones meant sunny weather. The rhyme, "Red sky at night, sailors delight. Red sky in the morning, sailors take warning," is probably the best-known example of traditional weather wisdom. Watch the sky and see if it is true.

## Weather Stations

A weather station is a facility where the weather and climate conditions is being observed. Meteorologists use different kinds of instruments to measure the temperature, pressure, humidity, wind speed, wind direction and precipitation amounts so as to be able to provide information for weather forecasts.

Weather Symbols

Weather Map

## Weather Maps and Symbols

A weather map presents various meteorological features across a particular region at a particular point in time. Weather symbols are used to denote each type of weather circumstance.

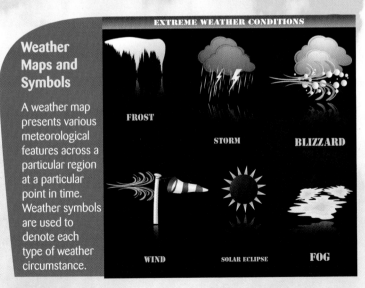

### EXTREME WEATHER CONDITIONS

FROST

STORM

BLIZZARD

WIND

SOLAR ECLIPSE

FOG

## Weather Satellites

A weather satellite is a type of satellite that is primarily used to monitor the weather and climate of the Earth. Humans send satellites into space to travel around the Earth. The satellites send back information to scientists on the ground. Some of the information they give us is about the weather and the Earth's temperature. Their cameras take pictures of clouds, the land, eyes in the sea storms, tornadoes and hurricanes. This information helps weather forecasters know predict the weather. The network of five satellites called 'metstats' provide a weather watch for the whole world. You can often see metstat pictures on television weather forecasts.

## Weather Balloons

Weather balloons carry special instruments that send all kinds of information about the weather back to people on the ground. Nearly 3000 weather balloons are launched into the air daily from different weather stations. These balloons are filled with hydrogen or helium and these send information about the weather changes to their respective stations.

# What is an Earthquake?

### Earthquake

An earthquake is the sudden shaking, trembling, quivering movement of the Earth's surface. While earthquakes usually last for not more than a minute, some can last longer and can cause devastating consequences. More than a million earthquakes rattle the world every year. Earthquakes are unpredictable although scientists who study earthquakes, called seismologists, have been trying to find out ways to do so. They can however be measured and recorded by an instrument called a seismometer. The richer scale was later developed to measure the magnitude and intensity of the earthquakes.

## What causes an earthquake?

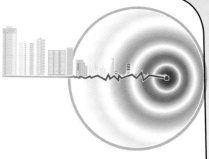

The Earth's crust is considered to be composed of several, large plates that move slowly past each other. These plates are called tectonic plates. Sometimes, these plates bump into each other or rather crash into each other causing the rocks to shift with great force. This area where two of these plates come together is called a fault. When this happens, it causes the crust to break. This brings about a movement in the Earth in the form of waves, making the ground shake and releasing an enormous form of energy, thereby causing an earthquake.

## Quick fact

The science devoted to the study of earthquakes is called seismology.

## Focus and epicentre

The focus of an earthquake is the area where the fault ruptures and the earthquake begins; the epicentre is the area on the surface located precisely above the earthquake's focus. If the epicentre is located near the sea, then it can cause the creation of tsunami waves.

# Why does the Earth Crack-up?

Earthquakes don't swallow people, animals or cars!

This is a common myth that has haunted civilizations since times immemorial. While cracks can form, usually caused by the up and down movements of the soil shifting the height of the soil, the Earth does not actually crack open and eat you up. Open ground cracks can form during an earthquake and if a person is standing at that exact spot where the earth is cracking, then that person could fall in.

Some cracks can be big. These cracks are called fault lines. Faults are caused when the shifting of plates, likely to cause an earthquake, cause stress on a layer of rock causing it to break and crack open. Geologists work hard at tracking down these fault lines. By finding their locations, they can locate the regions at risk of an earthquake taking place.

## Did you know?

When plates push up against each other, they create landslides, mountain ranges and even volcanoes! Mt. Everest was created in this way.

## Seaquakes and Tidal Waves

When the epicentre of an earthquake is located at the bottom of the ocean, it causes movements in the water that are perceptible at the surface. The waves that head toward the closest coastline are a little more than 1 m high. However, when the waves reach shallow waters, they start to grow up to 10 m high and when they slam into the shore, they cause tremendous damage. These huge tidal waves are called tsunamis. Underwater volcanic eruptions can also cause catastrophic tsunamis.

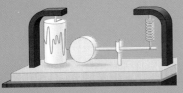

## What is a seismograph?

A seismograph is a device that records and measures the vibrations and movements of the earth during an earthquake. This helps the seismologists to estimate how powerful the earthquake was.

While seismologists cannot predict the earthquake, animals can. Animals can sense these waves before the actual earthquake takes place. Usually they become nervous and uneasy before an earthquake occurs.

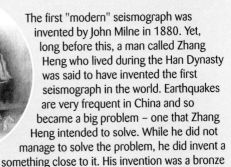

The first "modern" seismograph was invented by John Milne in 1880. Yet, long before this, a man called Zhang Heng who lived during the Han Dynasty was said to have invented the first seismograph in the world. Earthquakes are very frequent in China and so became a big problem – one that Zhang Heng intended to solve. While he did not manage to solve the problem, he did invent a something close to it. His invention was a bronze jar with eight small dragons resting on it, facing eight different directions. Each dragon had a ball balanced in its mouth. Whenever an earthquake took place, one dragon's mouth would open dropping the ball into the mouth of a waiting frog. This showed Zhang Heng which direction the earthquake was coming from.

# How to Read a Seismograph?

When an earthquake occurs somewhere under the surface of the Earth, shock waves are sent off in all directions.

Some of these waves compress the rock layers inside the Earth, and this compression wave, or 'P' wave, travels through the Earth, eventually to be recorded by the instruments.

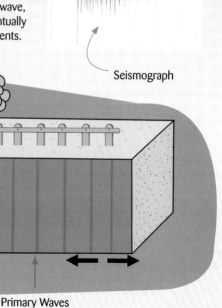

Seismograph

Primary Waves

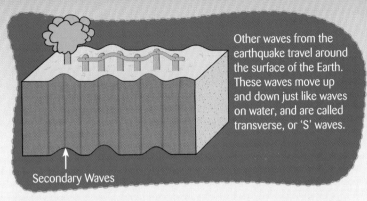

Other waves from the earthquake travel around the surface of the Earth. These waves move up and down just like waves on water, and are called transverse, or 'S' waves.

Secondary Waves

They're the ones that cause damage to things on the surface. Eventually these waves get to you too.

Since, the 'P' waves move a lot faster, so the seismograph will first record the 'P' waves from the earthquake. Later, when the 'S' waves arrive, it will record those too.

Folds caused in the rock due to the movement of Earth's surface.

# The Deadliest Earthquakes of the 21st Century

## Chile Earthquake, 2010

This earthquake occurred off the coast of the Maule Region of Chile on February 27, 2010.

It's magnitude was recorded to be 8.8 on the Richter scale and lasted for up to 3 minutes.

The earthquake triggered a tsunami which devastated several coastal towns in south-central Chile and damaged the port at Talcahuano.

The earthquake also generated a blackout that affected 93% of the country's population and which went on for several days in some locations.

## Indian Ocean, 2004

On December 26th 2004, a massive undersea earthquake hit the Indian Ocean, with an epicentre off the west coast of Sumatra, Indonesia.

The Earthquake had terrible effects and triggered a chain of devastating tsunamis along the coasts of most landmasses bordering the Indian Ocean.

With a magnitude of 9.1 on the Richter scale, it was the second largest earthquake ever recorded on a seismograph.

This earthquake lasted for about 8–10 minutes.

This earthquake, killed around 230, 000 people

### Gujarat Earthquake, 2001

The Gujarat earthquake occurred on January 26, 2001, India's 51st Republic Day.

The epicentre was Chobari Village in Bhachau Taluka of Kutch District of Gujarat, India.

With a magnitude of between 7.6 and 8.1 on the Richter scale, the quake killed around 20,000 people, injured another 167,000 and destroyed nearly 400,000 homes.

It was the second largest recorded earthquake in India.

## Japan Quake and Tsunami, 2011

A magnitude 9.0 earthquake hit the coast of Honshu, Japan on 11th March 2011. This led to the massive tsunami that was 10 meter in height and it swept away the entire towns, houses, almost everything in its path. The depth of the quake was almost 24.4 kms. Entire towns were wiped off the map, buildings washed away,highways collapsed,railway tracks were damaged and airports destroyed.

According to U.S. Geological Survey, this was the fifth biggest earthquake in the history of the world and the biggest ever for Japan.

Tsunami Wave

Kobe Earthquake, Japan

# What is a Volcano?

One of the most notable manifestations of the planet's activity is the eruption of volcanoes. There are different types of volcanoes, depending on how the lava is expelled, and they are located only in certain parts of the globe.

Volcano

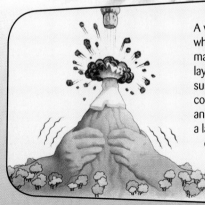

A volcano is a mountain where molten rocky material exits the interior layers of the Earth's surface. A volcano is covered in vents, craters and holes. At its peak is a large hole which opens downward to a pool of burning liquid rock.

Volcanic eruptions have had catastrophic effects to the regions to which it belongs. Eruptions have caused lateral blasts, hot ash flows, lava flows, mud slides and even avalanches. Around 1500 volcanoes are said to be on this Earth, out of these, 80 are said to be under the sea. An erupting volcano can cause earthquakes and tsunamis as it also involves movement within the Earth's surface.

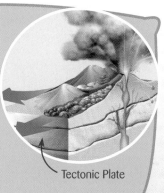

Tectonic Plate

### Did you know?

The name "volcano" has its origin from the name of Vulcan, a god of fire in Roman mythology.

Lava

# An Inside Look at the Earth

If we were to cut through our planet, we would find different layers beneath the crust. Each layer is wrapped around the other. The Earth is not a uniform rocky sphere but rather is made up of very dense materials that are found in different states and are distributed in characteristic ways. Inside the Earth, we would find three basic layers. They are the thin crust, the mantle beneath it and finally the core.

The innermost layer of the planet is not a dense, solid mass, as we might think; rather, it is in a semi liquid state in spite of the tremendous pressure that exists. Of the two parts that make it up, the inner one is denser.

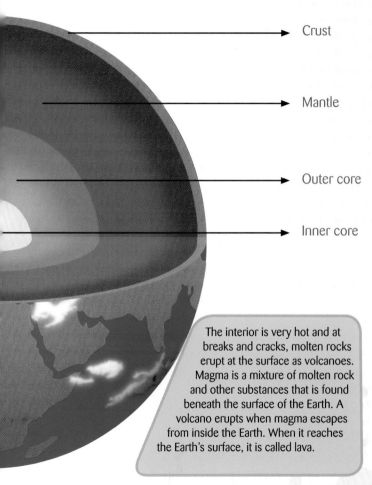

Crust

Mantle

Outer core

Inner core

The interior is very hot and at breaks and cracks, molten rocks erupt at the surface as volcanoes. Magma is a mixture of molten rock and other substances that is found beneath the surface of the Earth. A volcano erupts when magma escapes from inside the Earth. When it reaches the Earth's surface, it is called lava.

# Types of Volcanoes

### There are four types of Volcanoes:

An **active volcano** is a volcano that is erupting or has erupted recently and has the tendency to erupt again in the future. It can erupt anytime and these eruptions occur more often.

Mt. Kilauea, Hawaii

Mt. Etna

**Intermittent volcanoes** erupt at fairly regular time periods. Mount Asama, Mount Etna, and Hualalai are some intermittent volcanoes.

A **dormant volcano** is a volcano that is presently in an inactive state but may become active and erupt again. Mt. Merbabu in Indonesia is an example of dormant volcano.

Mt. Merababu, Indonesia

**Representation of the types of Volcanoes**

Mt. Kilimanjaro, Tanzania

Inactive volcanoes which have not erupted since the beginning of recorded history are **extinct volcanoes**.

161

# Volcanoes based on their Shapes

Mount Fuji, Japan

Mount Vesuvius, Italy

## Composite Volcanoes

Composite volcanoes are steep-sided volcanoes composed of many layers of volcanic rocks which are made from thick sticky lava, ash and rock debris. These are very tall and conical shaped volcanoes formed due to the hardening of lava, pumice and volcanic ash. Stratovolcanoes are characterized by a steep profile and periodic, explosive eruptions. It is characterized by the formation of a number of layers (strata) of hardened lava, volcanic ash and tephra, due to sequential outpourings of eruptive material. Since the magma is thick and sticky, the gas cannot escape and builds up inside the chamber until it explodes sending out huge clouds of burning rock and gas.

Ruins of Pompeii

Two most deadly examples of the composite volcanoes are Mount Fuji in Japan and Mount Vesuvius in Italy.

Dead body preserved in Pompeii

When Vesuvius erupted in AD79, it completely buried the town of Pompeii below, as well as devastating other nearby villages. The eruption column was a 20 mile tall spout of magma and rock. It kept erupting continuously for almost 20 hrs. Since then, the volcano has erupted over a dozen times, most recently in 1944, when several nearby villages were destroyed.

## Shield Volcanoes

These are very large in size and are characterized by shallow sloping sides. Shield volcanoes are shaped like a bowl or shield in the middle with long gentle slopes made by the hot flowing lava. This hot fluid lava flows very smoothly out of the mountain and flows down the sides and hence gives it the appearance of a 'warrior's shield'.

Mount Kilauea, Hawaii

163

Big Island, Hawaii

Since shield volcanoes are almost continuously erupting lava, they are gradually growing in size due to the accumulation of fluid lava. Because of this gradual buildup, these volcanoes are the largest volcanoes on the Earth. Shield volcanoes are composed mainly of basaltic lava. The most prominent characteristic feature of a shield volcano is the lava tubes that are the small cave-like structures formed due to the hardening of the continuously erupting lava.

Mt. Mauna Loa

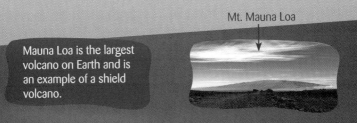

Mauna Loa is the largest volcano on Earth and is an example of a shield volcano.

The main examples include the volcanoes in Hawaii and Mount Etna. The volcano chain in the Hawaiian island is the most active and prominent example of a shield volcano.

### Extra Terrestrial Fact

Olympus Mons on Mars is also an example of a shield volcano.

## Did you know?

KILAUEA is the most active volcano on Earth. It is situated in Hawaii. This volcano has been erupting continuously for almost 25 years now since 1983!

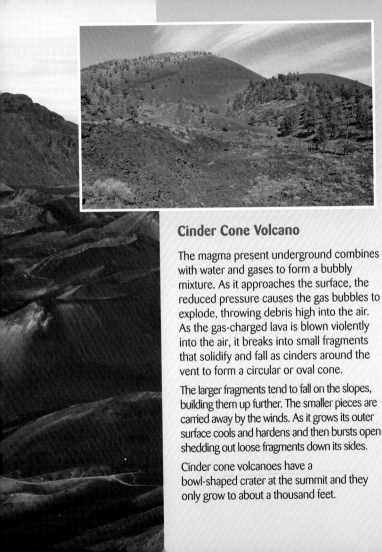

## Cinder Cone Volcano

The magma present underground combines with water and gases to form a bubbly mixture. As it approaches the surface, the reduced pressure causes the gas bubbles to explode, throwing debris high into the air. As the gas-charged lava is blown violently into the air, it breaks into small fragments that solidify and fall as cinders around the vent to form a circular or oval cone.

The larger fragments tend to fall on the slopes, building them up further. The smaller pieces are carried away by the winds. As it grows its outer surface cools and hardens and then bursts open shedding out loose fragments down its sides.

Cinder cone volcanoes have a bowl-shaped crater at the summit and they only grow to about a thousand feet.

## Lava Domes

Lava domes are formed by relatively small, bulbous masses of lava that are too viscous to flow any great distance. Lava domes are formed when erupting lava is very thick and is too viscous to flow. This leads to the formation of a steep-sided hill due to the accumulation of lava near the volcanic vent. The characteristic dome shape is attributed to high viscosity that prevents the lava from flowing very far. Domes may reach heights of several hundred meters, and can grow slowly and steadily for months, years, or even centuries.

The high viscosity of these domes can be attributed to the presence of high amounts of silica in the magma. The morphology of lava domes is variable. They are typically thick, steep extrusions, but their shapes can vary from circular, low-profile domes to cylindrical spines. Less sluggish types are gradational to lava flows and are sometimes referred to as dome flows . Lava domes have compositions ranging from basaltic andesite to rhyolite, although most are composed of crystal-rich dacite. Some lava domes erupt obsidian (volcanic glass), which forms when magma is cooled so quickly that individual minerals do not have time to crystallize.

St. Helens Volcano

# What are the Different Parts of a Volcano?

A volcano is a giant structure which is made up of many parts.

- **Eruption Cloud:** it is the cloud coming out from a volcano which contains ash and gases.
- **Pyroclastics:** these are the rock fragments.
- **Parasitic Cone:** a small cone-shaped volcano formed by an accumulation of volcanic debris.
- **Crater:** top of a volcano which surrounds the central vent and has widened over a number of eruptions.

- **Central Vent:** it is an opening at the top of a volcano through which magma erupts.

- **Conduit:** an underground passage or a long passage in the Earth through which magma travels upwards. It is also known as a feeder tube.

- **Side Vent:** it is a hole or a crack in Earth's surface that connects with the conduit. It also allows magma to erupt.

- **Lava:** the molten, fluid rock that issues from a volcano or volcanic vent.

- **Throat:** the throat is the upper part of the volcanic chimney during an eruption.

- **Magma Reservoir:** magma is the hot liquid rock and gases present in Earth's mantle or crust. This magma reservoir acts as a pool that feeds a volcano.

## Various stages of the volcanic eruption

# The Deadliest Volcanic Eruptions

## Mt. Erebus

It was discovered in 1841 by Sir James Clark Ross.

- Mount Erebus is the world's southernmost historically active volcano.
- The volcano is located on the western half of Ross Island.
- It was last active in 1991 and is one of only three active volcanoes in Antarctica.
- Erebus is noted for its convecting anorthoclase phonolite lava lake.
- Erebus is one of the volcanic seven summits.

## Magma System at Mount Erebus

Mt. Erebus volcano has a large and stable magma system. The volcano has persistent current activity. The composition of lava at the volcano has remained constant for the past 17,000 years.

## Mount Vesuvius, Italy

- Mount Vesuvius is a distinct hump-backed mountain, with a large cone that is partially encircled by the steep caldera.

- Mount Vesuvius is responsible for the destruction of the Roman cities of Herculaneum and Pompeii in AD 79. Both the cities were completely destroyed and covered with ash and pumice.

- When Vesuvius erupted, it covered the cities with 20 feet of volcanic debris.

- Mount Vesuvius is the only volcano within the Campanian Volcanic Arc to have erupted within recent history. It is the only active volcano on the European mainland.

- It last erupted in 1944.

## Laki, Iceland

- It is a legendary Icelandic volcano, which has lain dormant since its huge eruption in 1783.
- The Laki volcano eruption occurred in the June of 1783

in Iceland killing many thousands and spreading a massive haze that covered most of Europe and parts of North America.

- The 1725 meter, canyon-covered volcano caused nationwide damage when it spectacularly exploded, killing over 50% of the livestock population in Iceland at the time due to the clouds of poisonous fluorine and sulphur dioxide.

- The resulting famine killed 25% of the population.

- The repercussions of the Laki Volcano eruption in Iceland resonated throughout Europe for the next few years. The summer of 1783, having been turned to winter was followed by an extreme, harsh winter in 1784.

- In North America it was reported as one of the coldest on record.

Lakagigar, Iceland

## Papandayan, Indonesia

- Situated on the Indonesian island of Java, Papandayan is a semi-active volcano. It is a complex stratovolcano with four large summit craters.

- In 1772, one side of the volcano exploded and avalanched into the surrounding 40 villages, destroying them completely. Over 3,000 villagers were killed.

- After this eruption in 1772 the next major eruption that took place was in 2002, in which a crater wall collapsed.

- The volcano is still considered very dangerous and much of the surrounding area is restricted, especially considering there have been smoke, tremors and minor eruptions in 1923, 1942, and several others, all increasing in strength in 2002.

## Mt. Tambora, Indonesia

- Mt. Tambora erupted between April 10 - 15, 1816.

- Mt. Tambora, which was more than 13,000 feet tall before the explosion was reduced to 9,000 feet after ejecting more than 93 cubic miles of debris into the atmosphere.

- The eruption of Tambora killed an estimated 92,000 people, including 10,000 from explosion and ash fall, and 82,000 from other related causes.

- The concussion from the explosion was felt as far as a thousand miles away.

- The effects of the eruption were felt worldwide. 1816 became known as the "year without a summer" because of the volcanic ash in the atmosphere that lowered worldwide temperatures.

## The Eyjafjallajokull Glacier and Volcano in Southern Iceland

- The volcano erupted in March 2010. The ash cloud from the eruption had caused cancellation of flights all over the world.

- This eruption sent out a massive cloud of ash 20,000 feet into the air.

- The volcanic eruption of Eyjafjallajokull volcano partially melted a glacier, setting off a major flood that threatened to damage roads and bridges and forcing hundreds to evacuate from a thinly populated area.

- The volcano erupted twice in less than a month, melting ice, shooting smoke and steam into the air and forcing hundreds of people to flee due to rising floodwaters.

## Useful Words to Know

**Ash:** Fine particles of pulverized rock blown from an explosion vent.

**Epicentre:** It is the point directly above the focus or source of the earthquake.

**Magnitude:** A numerical expression of the amount of energy released by an earthquake, determined by measuring earthquake waves on seismographs.

**Primary Waves:** Waves that travel outward from an Earthquake's focus and cause particles in the rocks to move back and forth in the same direction the wave is moving.

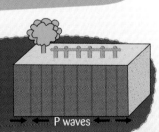

P waves

**Plate Tectonics:** The theory that the earth's crust is broken into about 10 fragments (plates) which move in relation to one another, shifting continents, forming new ocean crust, and stimulating volcanic eruptions.

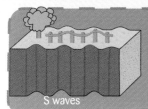

**Secondary Waves:** Waves that travel outward from an earthquake's focus and move through Earth by causing particles in the rocks to vibrate at right angles to the direction of the wave.

S waves

**Seismic Waves:** is the amount of energy released from the earthquake. These are the energy waves that are produced at and travel outward from the earthquake's focus.

**Asthenosphere:** The shell within the Earth, some tens of kilometres below the surface and of undefined thickness. It is a shell of weakness where plastic movements take place to permit pressure adjustments.

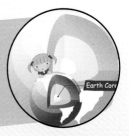

Earth Core

**Plate:** It may be defined as the individual sections of the lithosphere of the Earth. They fit together in a way similar to a jigsaw puzzle, but are always moving very slowly, floating on the molten rock of the lower mantle.

**Rhyolite:** Volcanic rock (or lava) that characteristically is light in colour, contains 69% silica or more, and is rich in potassium and sodium.

**Crater:** A steep-sided, usually circular depression formed by either explosion or collapse at a volcanic vent.

**Fault:** A crack or fracture in the Earth's surface. Movement along the fault can cause earthquakes.

**Tephra:** These are the bits of solidified rock or lava that are dropped from the air during an explosive eruption.

**Pumice Stone:** It is kind of volcanic rock that has been solidified. It is a light, porous, glassy lava in solidified form that is used as an abrasive.

**Seismologist:** Scientist who studies earthquakes.

**Seismometer:** It may be defined as the machine or an apparatus that receives seismic waves or impulses.

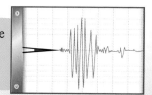

**Hot Geyser:** It is defined as the natural hot spring of water that keeps on ejecting water column and steam. These arise due to the result of volcanic activity.

# DISCOVERIES AND INVENTIONS

Curiosity and imagination have taken us to great heights. Mankind conquered the world around him, explored outer space and content in his own nest, he created a great number of inventions and discoveries that have played a big part in shaping our world.

As early as the classical Greek era, mathematicians had made calculations that suggested that our planet was a sphere. The idea that it was flat persisted well into the Middle Ages.

When Columbus undertook his voyage from Palos de Moguer, he was convinced that it was indeed possible to reach Asia by circumnavigating the globe – this would only be possible if one believed that the Earth was round and there were many people during that time who were still doubtful.

Years later, Magellan became the first man to circumnavigate the globe, turning what was once a thought into a fact. After that, the great journeys of discovery made it possible to formulate a more precise idea of what the world was really like making it possible to draw an accurate picture of the landmasses surrounded by a great expanse of water that together make up the planet Earth.

# Famous Explorers

## Ferdinand Magellan

Ferdinand Magellan was a Portuguese explorer and is credited for circumnavigating the Earth for the first time.

## Amerigo Vespucci

Amerigo Vespucci was the Italian explorer and navigator, and also one of the early explorers of the New World. It is generally believed that America got its name from his Latin name Americus Vespucci.

## Hernan Cortes

Hernan Cortes was a Spanish conquistador and explorer. He is best known for conquering the Mexico and the Aztec Empire.

## James Cook

James Cook was a great explorer because he was the first to lead a sailing expedition around the world successfully. He commanded the 'Endeavor' on his first trip to the Pacific, an expedition to observe Venus for the Royal Society. He landed at Tahiti and became the first European to discover and chart the coasts of New Zealand, Australia, and New Guinea. On another three-year voyage, Cook explored the ice fields of Antarctica.

## William Dampier

William was an explorer and sea captain, and is one of the most highly regarded map-makers and navigators of all time. Dampier led several voyages of mapping and exploration around the world. He was the first Englishman to explore or map parts of New Holland, Australia and New Guinea. He was also the first person to circumnavigate the world thrice.

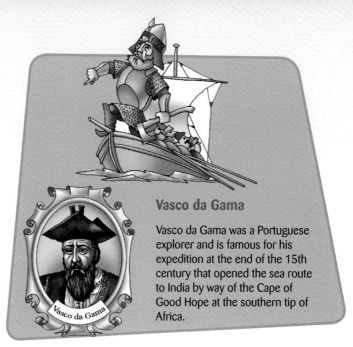

## Vasco da Gama

Vasco da Gama was a Portuguese explorer and is famous for his expedition at the end of the 15th century that opened the sea route to India by way of the Cape of Good Hope at the southern tip of Africa.

## Francis Drake

Sir Francis Drake was a British explorer and slave-trader. Francis Drake achieved lasting fame as a result of his association with the victory against the Spanish Armada. He was a loyal subject of Queen Elizabeth I. From 1577 to 1580, Drake circumnavigated the world.

## Discovery of America

The American continent was discovered by Christopher Columbus. His objective was to sail to Asia (the Indies) where the riches of gold, pearls and spice were present in abundance. In 1484 the Portuguese were already working on a way to Asia and rejected Christopher's theories.

Columbus moved to Spain for permission but faced rejections from the Spanish royal commission as well. His hard work finally paid off on April 1492 when Ferdinand V, king of Castile, and Queen Isabella agreed to sponsor his expedition. Columbus led his three ships, namely the Nina, the Pinta and the Santa Maria out of the Spanish port on August 3, 1492.

He first sailed to the Canary Islands, where he stayed for a month, and then he started the five week voyage across the ocean. It is said that Columbus faked the logbook to make his crew believe they had covered a smaller distance than they actually had!

The Pinta

### Did You Know?

When Christopher Columbus reached America, he was convinced that he was in India. That is why the natives of America were called Indians.

Christopher Columbus never knew that he had discovered a new country. Till the day he died he thought that he had reached India.

# A Stroke of Luck

> Louis Pasteur once said that chances favour the prepared minds.

## Popsicle

Many people don't know this but the invention of the popsicle was purely accidental. It was invented by an eleven year old boy named Frank Epperson.

One day, he had left his fruit flavoured soda outside on the porch with a stirring stick in it. He left the mixture on the back porch overnight and the next day Frank found that the drink froze to the stick.

And this was how the popsicle came about.

## Microwave

Dr. Percy Spencer was working as an engineer with the Raytheon Corporation. While he was testing a new vacuum tube called a magnetron, he found that the candy bar in his pocket had melted.

Out of curiosity, Dr. Spencer decided to test it once again. He placed some corn kernels near the tube and he saw that the corn popped all over his lab.

The Raytheon Corporation developed the first commercial microwave oven in 1947.

### Ice Cream Cone

Did you know that an ice cream cone is made the same way as a waffle?

Ernest Hamwi created the first ice cream cone for serving ice cream in 1904 at the St. Louis World's Fair. His waffle booth was next to an ice cream vendor who ran short of dishes. Hamwi rolled a waffle and scooped icecream into it. This was the beginning of the ice cream cone.

## Champagne

There was once a poor wine maker called Dom Perignon. He had spent two years trying to make sparkling wine. Instead he ended up making a unique tasting drink loaded with bubbles. Little did he know that this drink, which we know of as champagne would become one of the world's most popular drink!

### Did you know?

The sparkling bubbles in the champagne were considered to be some kind of impurity or fault initially.

# Post-it Notes

No one ever planned on inventing post-it-notes, it just happened. And surprisingly, it turned out to be one of the handiest creations of the 21st century.

This all happened one day when a chemist, named Spencer Silver was working on improving an adhesive. While he started off trying to make the glue stronger, he accomplished the exact opposite, making it less sticky instead. Well, the experiment didn't work as expected, so he kept it away.

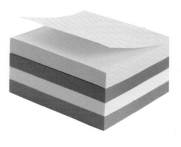

One day, a colleague of his', named Arthur Fry, was at church. He used paper markers to keep his place in the hymnal but they just kept falling off. Suddenly an ingenious idea popped into his mind! He used Spencer Silver's glue to stick the markers to the paper. The glue was strong enough to hold the paper together, but still not strong enough to maintain the bond when pulled on.

Soon after, the company which they were both working for began distributing post-it-notes nationwide.

# Potato Chips

Can you imagine a world without potato chips?

Potato chips originated from potato fries, as you would have already guessed. One day, a chef, named George Crum, employed at an elegant resort in New York grew tired of a guest complaining about the quality of his fried potatoes. They were too "thick, soggy and bland" according to the guest. Crum, agitated, decided to slice this potato fries as thin as possible, fried them till they became crispy and added extra salt to it. The guest loved the fries and soon the dish gained popularity came to be known worldwide. And that is how we have the potato chips!

# Penicillin

More than an invention, penicillin was rather a discovery. One day, a young physician, Alexander Fleming, left a bacteria-smeared culture plate on his lab. Fleming was trying to find out ways to cure many diseases that killed many people back in the day. Back then, people died from very small and minor wounds and illnesses. Two weeks later, he found that a mould had developed in the bacteria-smeared culture plate. He noticed that the area around the mould, there was no bacteria. He had discovered penicillin! Penicillin came to be one of the greatest discoveries of all-time. It was used to create antibiotics, curing people of many different kinds of diseases and giving the sick a chance at life.

## Did you know?

Thousands of years ago, before the invention of penicillin, the Chinese used soybean curd, which had mould to cure boils and many types of skin infections. This means that even before the discovery and use of penicillin, mould was used to cure many types of injuries!

# Making Life Easy

Imagine a world without the telephone or the postage stamp. Getting in touch with friends and family would be extremely difficult. Picture a world where there was no telescope – we would not know much that we know now about space and its wonders. Imagine living in a world where mankind had no imagination and he never thought of better things. Indeed, we take such things for granted. These are the inventions that have altered the face of the world.

Prof. Bell's vibrating reed–used for a receiver

Alexander Graham Bell's first telephone

## Did you know?

Bell never considered the telephone as a great work. Instead he thought of it as a disturbance to his real work as a scientist.

## Telephone

While the telegraph was years in use, the telephone came much later and started off as an improvement of the telegraph. Alexander Graham Bell, a name that has been and shall continue to be remembered throughout the ages invented the telephone. He, along with his companion worked together at creating a device that could transmit speech through sound. In 1875, Bell and Watson invented one of the world's greatest inventions – the telephone.

## Ball-point Pen

People have used many different items to produce ink on paper. They first used brushes, then they used feathers, then they used metallic pens with nibs and finally they used the fountain pen. Laszlo Biro however, a journalist, grew tired of using the fountain pen as the ink would spill frequently. He noticed that the ink that is used for printing newspapers was very thick and dried quickly. But the ink was simply too thick. He fitted his pen with a tiny metallic ball at its tip. This ball rotated when he moved it along the paper, picking up ink from the cartridge and leaving it on the paper. Finally Laszlo Biro and the rest of the world could produce neat, tidy and smudge free writing on paper!

## First Artificial Refrigerator

Before the invention of the refrigerator, people transported ice from cold and mountainous regions to preserve their food. The Chinese, Greeks and Romans alike all adopted this practice. They preserved the ice in pits or caves shielded with straw and wood. This provided them with a supply of ice for months. In the year 1748, the first artificial refrigerator was created by William Cullen, who simply improved on this age old practice. And because of him, we no longer have to transport ice from different regions in order to be able to store food!

## Postage Stamp

During the 18th century, sending letters to people by post was extremely expensive. A Victorian reformer, Rowland Hill, who lived during that time, reformed the British postal system by inventing the postal stamp. At that time when letters were being sent, it was the recipient who had to bear the cost and not the sender. Rowland Hill attempted to reverse that role. The penny black became the world's first postal stamp where the postage fee would be paid by the sender and not the recipient. The penny black postage stamp became the first postage stamp to be used in a public postal system.

The introduction of envelopes was also another important step at reforming the British postal system. Back then, sending letters was very expensive as it was priced according to the number of sheets a person used and distance to which it travelled. This altered the previous system of calculating postage and made it accessible to all.

### Did you know?

Not only did Rowland Hill invent the postage stamp, but he also introduced the use of envelopes to enclose the letters.

Before 1800 BC, alphabets were not in use. The Egyptians wrote using pictures inscribed on stone. These were called hieroglyphs. After 1800 BC, people from Canaan, which is now Israel and Lebanon travelled to Egypt. They did not know how to read and write and found the Egyptian writings interesting. But learning the Egyptian way of writing was too difficult. So, they decided to have their own, formulating simpler versions of the Egyptian hieroglyphs. This is where the first version of the alphabet came from.

The alphabet has been considered to be the first of inventions and the greatest too, opening up knowledge and communication to the world.

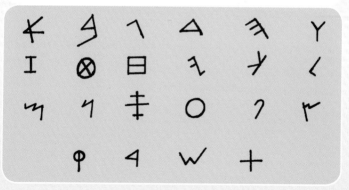

### Let's not forget the wheel!

One of mankind's first inventions, the wheel has actually been around for nearly as long as man himself. The invention of the wheel dates too far back for us to have any record of its inventor (if he or she ever had a name), but research has shown that it was first invented by the Mesopotamians sometime around 8,000 BC. Pretty old huh?

The first wheel was said to have been made by joining together planks of wood and rolling it on the ground with a cart on top. This discovery is the first of many as it ushered in other great inventions from automobiles to aeroplanes, to factory machines and many others.

## Atomic Bomb

J. Robert Oppenheimer was born in New York City. Oppenheimer was the son of German immigrants and textile importers.

When World War II began, Oppenheimer eagerly became involved in the efforts to develop an atomic bomb, which were already taking up much of the time and facilities of Lawrence's Radiation Laboratory at Berkeley.

199

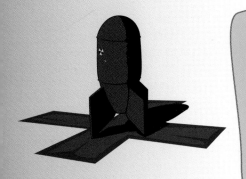

He was invited to take over work on neutron calculations, and in June 1942 General Leslie Groves appointed Oppenheimer as the scientific director of the Manhattan Project.

The joint work of the scientists at Los Alamos resulted in the first nuclear explosion at Alamagordo on July 16, 1945, which Oppenheimer named "Trinity."

## Telescope

The first man to look into space was the man who created the telescope. His name was Galileo Galilei. While the telescope was created before Galilei by various optical lens makers, they could not really make proper use of it. Galilei was the first man who introduced it to astronomy, making it one of the world's greatest inventions, paving the way for mankind to discover the wonders of space. Also, the telescope he invented could see further and clearer than all the others in the market. Through this device, he became the first man to see the craters of the moon; he discovered sunspots and was the first person to observe the majestic rings of Saturn. It was through the telescope that he was able to establish that the Earth along with all the planets revolved around the Sun.

### Did you know?

Galileo Galilei first created this invention so that he would be able to sell it to the Venetian authorities so that it could be used as a spyglass to be able to catch pirates who were taking over or stole from their ships.

# Inventions Named after People

## Sandwich – Earl of Sandwich

The term "sandwich" originated in 1762 in London, while slices of bread with meat and cheese had been eaten since the dawn of the loaf of bread.

One night, an English nobleman, John Montagu, the 4th Earl of Sandwich was busy gambling. He did not stop for a meal despite being hungry.

Legend has it that John Montagu called for such a dish to be served to him, so he could remain at the gaming table without breaking for supper.

This incident gave us the quick-food product that we now know as the sandwich.

## Saxophone – Adolphe Sax

The saxophone was invented by Antoine Joseph Adolphe Sax, a Belgian musical instrument designer.

Adolphe's first important invention was an improvement of the bass clarinet design which he patented at the age of twenty-four.

In 1840, Sax invented the clarinette-bourdon, an early design of contrabass clarinet. He developed the saxophone instrument during this period and patented it in 1846.

The saxophone was invented for use in both orchestras and concert bands.

203

## Diesel Engine - Rudolf Diesel

Rudolf Diesel was born in Paris on March 18, 1858.

While an employee of the Linde firm, Diesel became fascinated with the theoretical work of the French physicist Nicholas Carnot, which presented the principles of the modern internal combustion engine.

Rudolf Diesel designed many heat engines, including a solar-powered air engine. In 1893, he published a paper describing an engine with combustion within a cylinder, the internal combustion engine. In 1894, he filed for a patent for his new invention, named as diesel engine. His engine was the first to prove that fuel could be ignited without a spark. He operated his first successful engine in 1897.

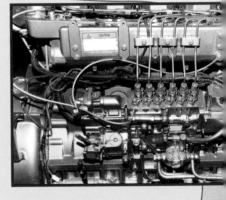

## Nikola Tesla

Nikola Tesla as a child was exceptionally gifted. He often watched his mother work hard to introduce new things to lighten her chores. This encouraged him to think out of the box and innovate a number of technical discoveries. In his lifetime, he successfully created the Tesla induction coil, electromagnetic motors, remote control, radio and fluorescent lightning.

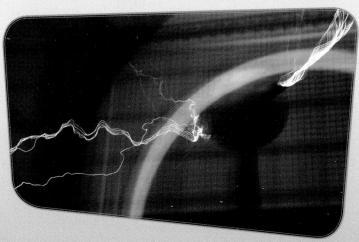

# Inventors Killed by their Own Inventions

**84**

2
8
18
32
18
6

# Po

Polonium
(208.9824)

**88**

2
8
18
32
18
8
2

# Ra

Radium
(226)

## Marie Curie (1867–1934)

Marie Curie was the first lady professor to be honoured with two Nobel prizes. She pioneered the work conducted on radioactive elements. She spent many years conducting research for the treatment of the fatal disease – cancer. While doing so, the continuous exposure to radiation led her to her death.

## Franz Reichelt (1879–1912)

Franz Reichelt was an Austrian tailor who designed an overcoat that would act as a parachute.

Reichelt was known by the locals as the flying tailor.

He used his skills as a tailor to create an overcoat that he was sure would allow him to fly, glide or float to the ground without harm.

He demonstrated his invention with his only jump of 60 meters from the first deck of the Eiffel Tower.

This turned out to be a disaster and he died.

### Alexander Bogdanov

Alexander Bogdanov was a Russian physician, economist, philosopher, natural scientist, writer and polymath who wrote science fiction books.

He believed that blood transfusions could extend life and rejuvenate health. He was the founder of the world's first institution devoted entirely to the field of blood transfusion. In 1924, Bogdanov started his blood transfusion experiments, apparently hoping to achieve eternal youth or at least partial rejuvenation.

He gave himself 11 blood transfusions and was very satisfied. But the twelfth transfusion cost him his life, when he took the blood of a student suffering from malaria and tuberculosis.

## William Bullock

William Bullock was born in Greenville, New York in 1813. He invented the web rotary printing press.

William Bullock's invention, in 1863, represents the beginning of the modern, web-fed newspaper press, which works from curved, stereotype plates and prints on both sides of the paper in one pass through the machine.

On April 3, 1867, Bullock tried to kick a driving belt onto a pulley while making some adjustments in his new press and he crushed his leg. After a few days, he developed gangrene and died on 12th April, 1867.

# Greatest Discoveries of All Time

Millions of years of mankind's existence on the Earth have resulted in the discovery and invention of innumerable wonders and untold knowledge. These have all worked together at shaping the world that we live in. Here are some of the greatest discoveries and inventions of all time – having altered the face of the Earth completely.

## The Sun is the Centre of the Solar System

When man first began his journey on Earth, he did not know where the Sun, the Earth, the moon or the stars came from. He wondered in awe and curiosity. He did not know of the existence of the Solar system and for a long time believed that the Earth was the centre of the Universe.

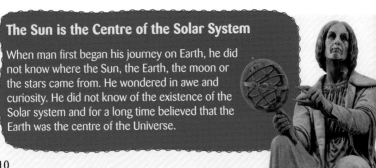

Triqetrum used by Copernicus

A Greek philosopher and astronomer, Aristarchus of Samos was the first to propose his theory that the Earth was not the centre of the Universe and that it revolved around the Sun. But, before that, great men like Ptolemy and Aristotle had laid claim that the Earth was the centre of the Universe so his ideas, with no means of finding out the truth, were rejected.

Nicolaus Copernicus delved more into this idea and was the first man to formulate a comprehensive and detailed theory that the Earth was not the centre of the Universe.

Years later, Galileo Galilei observed this fact through his telescope.

## Micro-organisms

Antony van Leeuwenhoek, a Dutch cloth merchant, was the first person to see bacteria. During the 1660s he started to grind glass lenses to make better magnifying lenses so he could examine the weave of cloth more easily. He excelled at lens grinding and achieved magnifications up to 500 times life-size. He used his best lens to look at a sample of pond water, and saw that it was teeming with tiny living things. It was he who discovered bacteria, free-living and parasitic microscopic protists, sperm cells, blood cells, microscopic nematodes and rotifers, and much more.

## Gravity

Legend has it that one day, as Sir Isaac Newton was sitting under an apple tree reading a book, an apple fell on his head. He picked up the apple and wondered why the apple had to fall down at all. Why couldn't it have fallen up? Have you ever wondered why things fall down rather than fall up? Even when we throw things upward, they come back down.

According Sir Isaac Newton, there is such a force called gravity which holds the universe together. There is a gravitational force between any two objects in the universe, so it is called universal gravitation. Gravity pulls us down because there is a gravitational force between us and the Earth.

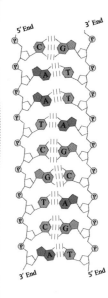

## DNA: Deoxyribonucleic Acid

DNA was first identified in the late 1860s by Swiss chemist Friedrich Miescher. The discovery of DNA shaped our understanding of genetics, leading to applications in the field of forensics, genetic engineering and so on.

On April 1953, James Watson and Francis Crick presented the structure of the DNA-helix, the molecule that carries genetic information from one generation to the other. They proposed that the DNA molecule exists in the form of a three-dimensional double helix.

## Hot Air Balloons

We have learnt that hot air is lighter than cold air. Two brothers named Joseph and Etienne Montgolfer discovered this and drew up a plan to invent a small silk balloon.

Burning straw, wool and dried horse manure was kept underneath the balloon. This caused the heat inside the balloon to heat up, inflating the balloon and causing it to rise. When it was first launched, it rose to a height of 500 feet.

### Did you know?

The first passengers to fly in a hot air balloon were a sheep, a duck and a rooster.

215

# Wonder Drugs

## Cure for Malaria

In the ancient times, malarial fever was one of the many diseases that claimed many lives. Many methods were tried out to cure this disease like operations and amputations but none of them seemed to work. The indigenous people of Peru however had their own methods. They used the bark of the cinchona tree to control it. Years later, the Spanish Jesuit missionaries in Peru took note of the effectiveness of the practice and introduced it to Europe.

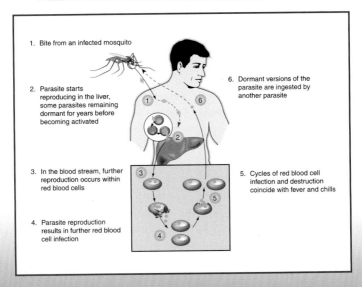

1. Bite from an infected mosquito

2. Parasite starts reproducing in the liver, some parasites remaining dormant for years before becoming activated

3. In the blood stream, further reproduction occurs within red blood cells

4. Parasite reproduction results in further red blood cell infection

5. Cycles of red blood cell infection and destruction coincide with fever and chills

6. Dormant versions of the parasite are ingested by another parasite

In the year 1820, the active ingredient called quinine which was needed to cure the disease was extracted from the bark and used to make medicines. During that time, studies were also going on regarding the cause of the disease. By the 20th century, scientists had discovered the cause of the disease which was transmitted through mosquito bites and the medicine came to be known and accepted worldwide.

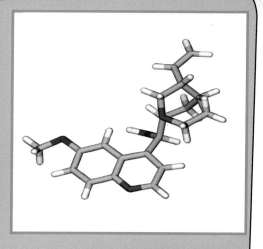

The cinchona tree, also known as quina quina, gives the drug quinine, which has been used for the cure of malaria ever since.

## Aspirin

Long before the manufacture of aspirin came about, sometime in 400 BC, the "father of modern medicine," Hippocrates prescribed the bark of leaves of the willow tree to relieve pain and fever. This was rich in a substance called salicin. In the year 1832, German chemists experimented with the bark and created salicylic acid. By 19th century, aspirin had been developed and was sold worldwide.

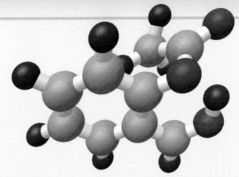

Although it started as a medicine for pain relief, it later became noted for other benefits too. In 1948, a medical practitioner observed that patients taking aspirin regularly had lesser risks of having a heart attack. Now aspirin is considered the number one drug in the world.

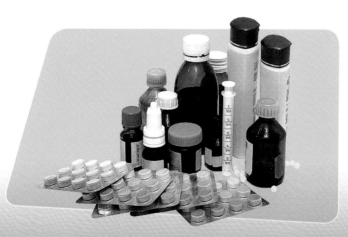

# Light Bulb Moments

### Aeroplane

When they were young boys, Wilbur and Orville Wright received a gift from their father which would change their lives forever. It was a miniature toy plane, powered by a rubber band. How great this impacted their lives can be seen by their greatest creation – the aeroplane, accomplishing mankind's lifelong dream – the dream of flight.

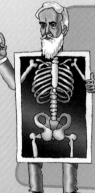

### X-Ray

Like most other discoveries, this too was accidental.

A German physicist, Wilhelm Conrad Röntgen is credited for the discovery of x-rays.

Wilhelm Röntgen was conducting experiments in his laboratory on the effects of cathode rays when he discovered X-rays in 1895.

Röntgen described a new form of radiation that allowed him to photograph objects that were hidden behind opaque shield.

## Bone China

Before bone china came to be invented, most porcelain was made and exported from China. At that time, importing porcelain from China was very expensive. Around the year 1800, a famous potter started working at improving this creation. He combined the ash of animal bone with the other ingredients used to make porcelain and created what we know as bone china. Bone china is now a desired collectable, priced at high rates and the most preferred choice for dinnerware.

## Textile

The creation of textile dates back to the ancient times where fibre was being used to create cloth. The first recorded use of fibre was sometime during the 6th and 7th Centuries by the Swiss lake inhabitants. They created wool and flax fabric. Yet, the first actual textile was believed to have been made of felt. Other countries like China, India, Turkey, Persia and many more also had a rich textile tradition. The aristocracy adorned themselves with luxurious woven silk. The art of weaving and spinning was practiced by innumerable cultures. It was until the 18th century, when the industrial revolution came about that machines were being used for creating textiles. Various other synthetic fibres were created soon after paving the way for a wide market.

## Printing Press

The earliest forms of printing were found to have started before 3000 BC where images were impressed on clay tablets by the early Mesopotamian civilization. The civilizations of China and Egypt made use of small stamps used as seals. Printing on cloth was practiced in India and Europe. It was in the year 1440 that a goldsmith named German Johannes Gutenberg invented the world's first moveable printing system which revolutionised the entire printing process.

## Blue Jeans

In the 16th century, sailors from Italy wore trousers made of a strong cloth like "jeans". The material "denim" had been created in England during the same time. In the year 1849, during the Gold Rush in America, a businessman started a small company which manufactured trousers out of this "denim" cloth. The businessman wanted to sell it to gold miners who wanted trousers that were strong and did not tear easily. Little did he know that he had created one of the most popular clothing in the world!

# INDEX

**A**

aeroplane 198, 220
Aldrin, Edwin 80
alphabet 197
anemometer 142
Apollo Mission 79
    Apollo 11 80
Aristarchus 211
Aristotle 66, 211
Armstrong, Neil 80, 81
aspirin 218, 219
asteroid 22, 23
asteroid belt 19
Atlantic Ocean 104
atmosphere 85, 111, 112, 114
atomic bomb 199-198

**B**

ball-point pen 195
barometer 115, 142
Bell, Graham 194
big bang theory 13
biodiversity 87
blizzard 114, 137
blood transfusions 208
bone china 221

**C**

canyons 102, 103
caves 101, 106, 164
champagne 190
climate 112, 113
    climate change 86
clouds 116-117
Columbus, Christopher 128,
    181, 186-187
comets 15, 22, 23, 29
Cook, James 184
Copernicus, Nicholas 68,
    69, 211
coral reefs 87, 108
core 32, 36, 158

Cortes, Hernan 183
craters 30, 31, 34, 40, 59,
    156, 211
crust 32, 36, 158-159
Curie, Marie 206

**D**

da Gama, Vasco 185
Dampier, William 184
desert 95
    oasis 95
diesel engine 204
dna 214
doldrums 130
doppler radar 138
downburst 138
Drake, Francis 185
drizzle 120

**E**

Earth 24, 28, 29, 38-39, 43,
    85-87
    biodiversity 87
    blue planet 39
eclipse 16-17
    lunar eclipse 16
    solar eclipse 17
epicentre 147, 149
erosion 91, 100, 101, 107
Esnault-Pelterie, R 72

**F**

fault lines 184
Fleming, Alexander 193
focus 147
fog 114, 122, 125
fog bow 125
fold mountains 89
frost 122

**G**

galaxy 14, 19, 39
Galilei, Galileo 14, 65, 69,
    201, 211
geysers 106
glacier 92, 107, 175

Goddard, R. H 73
grasslands 94, 96, 113
graupel 121
greenhouse effect 37, 86

**H**

hailstones 123
hieroglyphs 197
hot air balloons 215
hurricanes 114, 132, 135,
    136, 145
hygrometer 114

**I**

ice cream cone 189
icebow 126
Indian Ocean 131, 136, 153,
    104
islands 102

**J**

jeans 222
Jupiter 19, 22, 25, 28, 29,
    44-47, 62, 69, 83

**L**

lakes 22, 59, 89, 107
land breeze 131
lava 34, 156, 157, 159
light year 13, 14
lightning 114, 132, 133

**M**

Magellan, Ferdinand 181, 182
malaria 216-217
mangroves 87, 99
mantle 32, 36, 158
Mariner 2,4,X-34,42,33
marshes 99
meteorite showers 15
Mercury 19, 22, 23, 24, 28,
    29, 30-33
meteorologists 142, 143
micro-organisms 212
microwave oven 189
Milky way 14, 19, 69

moonbow 126
mountains 89, 90, 92, 100, 101, 102, 103

**N**
NASA 60, 77, 79, 82
Neptune 19, 22, 26, 28, 29, 56-59, 63, 83
Newton, Sir Isaac 213
northern forests 97

**O**
Oberth, Hermann 73
ocean currents 140-141
    Coriolis effect 140
oceans 22, 39, 103-105
    bottom plane 103
    continental shelf 103
    continental slope 103
    deep sea trenches 103
Olympus Mons 43, 165

**P**
Pacific Ocean 104, 184
penicillin 193
planetary systems 23
    dwarf planet 22, 23, 26, 27, 60-61
    gaseous planets 28
    moons 62-63
    rocky planets 28
plateau 101
Pluto 26, 27, 60
polar winds 130
post-it-notes 191
printing press 209, 222
psychrometer 114
Ptolemaeus, Claudius (Ptolemy) 67, 211

**R**
radiation 89, 199, 206, 220
rain 90, 105, 106, 113, 116, 118, 120, 121, 123, 132 142
rain forests 93

rain gauge 119, 142
rainbow 125
refrigerator 195
richer scale 146
rivers 22, 90, 92, 102, 105
rockets 70, 73, 74, 75, 78

**S**
sandstorm 139
satellites 82, 142, 145
Saturn 19, 22, 25, 28, 29, 48-51, 63, 201
savannas 94, 96
saxophone 203
sea breeze 131, 132
seaquakes and tidal waves 149
seasons 39, 112, 113
seismograph 150
seismologists 146, 150, 179
seismometer 146, 179
sleet 120
snow 92, 98, 105, 114, 119
    snowflake 119
solar system 13, 19-63, 82, 85, 210,
    evolution 21-23
space race 73-75
springs 95, 106
Sun 14, 17, 19, 21, 23
swamps 99

**T**
Tsiolkowski, K. E. 72
tectonic plates 47
telephone 194
telescope 14, 46, 48, 50, 52, 69, 194, 201, 211
Tesla, Nikola 205
textile 221
thermometer 115, 142
thunderstorm 132-135, 137, 138
tornadoes 132, 134, 137, 145, 112, 114
trade winds 132
troposphere 114

tsunami 139, 147, 149, 153, 155, 157
tundra 98

**U**
underground water 106
Uranus 19, 22, 25, 28, 29, 52-55, 63, 83

**V**
valleys 90, 100, 101, 102
Venus 19, 22, 23, 24, 28, 29, 34-37, 83, 184
Verne, Jules 71
Vespucci, Amerigo 183
volcanoes 22, 34, 103, 148, 149, 156-179
    formation 158-159
    parts 168-169
    shapes 162-167
    types 160-161
Von Braun, Wernher 72

**W**
waterfalls 105
waterspouts 136-137
Watson, Thomas. A 194
weather 111-145
    atmospheric pressure 114-115
    humidity 114, 143
    precipitation 118-124
    temperature 114-115
    weather and climate forecasting 142-145
westerlies 130
wetlands 99
wheel 198
whirlpools 105
whirlwinds 135, 136
wind vane 142
woodlands 97
Wright, Orville 220
Wright, Wilbur 220

**X**
x-rays 220